MW01519140

Susan Schept

The Voice of Sarah

Feminist Ethics in Jewish Sacred Text

Hadassa Word Press

Imprint
Any brand names and product names mentioned in this book are subject to trademark, brand or patent protection and are trademarks or registered trademarks of their respective holders. The use of brand names, product names, common names, trade names, product descriptions etc. even without a particular marking in this work is in no way to be construed to mean that such names may be regarded as unrestricted in respect of trademark and brand protection legislation and could thus be used by anyone.

Cover image: www.ingimage.com

Publisher:
Hadassa Word Press
is a trademark of
International Book Market Service Ltd., member of OmniScriptum Publishing Group
17 Meldrum Street, Beau Bassin 71504, Mauritius

Printed at: see last page
ISBN: 978-3-639-79527-1

Contents

Introduction 1

   An Overview of the Book 5

Chapter 1. How Jews Study Text 9

   The Sacred Texts 12

Chapter 2. Object Relations Theory, Neuroscience and Care Ethics ... 16

   Care Ethics 21

Chapter 3. The Feminine-Relationship-Interdependence 27

   The Primacy of Relationship 28

   Ona'at Devarim 29

   Hesed 31

Chapter 4. Justice and Compassion 38

   Noah and *Tsedek* 40

   Tsedakah 41

   Strict Justice and Going Beyond the Letter of the Law 41

   Compassion and Mercy 45

   Forgiveness 48

Chapter 5. Autonomy Within A Relational Context 51

   Autonomy: Individual and Relational 53

   The Oven of Akhnai 53

   Ma Tovu 54

   Tower of Babel 55

   Geneivat Da'at 56

Chapter 6. *Ezer K'negedo*, Moses, *Hevrutah* Study 59

   Moses 62

   Empathy 65

Chapter 7. Conclusion 69

BIBLIOGRAPHY 74

INDEX 77

Acknowledgements

I wish to express my gratitude to the following people for their inspiration, support and encouragement throughout this project: Dr. Jane Statlander-Slote without whom this endeavor would not have either come into existence or to fruition, Dr. Rachel Kidron for her insightful comments, Dr. Judah Schept and Dr. Andrew Rubenfeld for their expert editorial assistance, Dr. Michael Slote for his support and commentary, and special thanks to Dr. Susan Kavaler-Adler.

I also wish to acknowledge my very wonderful and supportive family: my husband, Ken and my children Judah, Rebecca and Brooke. I dedicate this book to my granddaughters Talula and Rhea, who continually give me hope for our future.

Introduction

A significant intellectual void exists in the culture at large when it comes to understanding and interpreting Jewish sacred text. Misconceptions of major Jewish concepts of justice, compassion, and the very nature of God exist even among Jews. This book will attempt to fill this void by delineating and describing the fundamentally linked characteristics of justice, care, and pity that are the very building blocks of Judaic thought and form the cornerstones of Western civilization. That these Jewish concepts have much in common and may even be considered the antecedents of modern feminist ideas regarding the nature of what is known as care ethics and foundational to what constitutes "self" is the theme that lies at the core of this text. Note that I am here construing "feminism" in the sense of looking and listening to women's voices and highlighting interpretations that have long been neglected. As will be further elucidated in the text, the feminine voice is the voice of relationship, the voice that emanates from a self that is constituted by and emerges from its primal relationships. It is my contention that it is a voice that is elevated in Jewish sacred text.

The misunderstandings and misconceptions are of an historic nature and have continued to the modern age. Examples abound: the writer Joseph Campbell speaking to Bill Moyers during one of the former's series of programs, "The Power of Myth," reiterated a frequently purveyed notion of the so-called "Old Testament" God as one of wrath and stern judgment who metes out justice with an iron hand. As Campbell quips "Computers are like Old Testament gods; lots

1

of rules and no mercy."[1] In like measure, the avowed atheist, Oxford University's Richard Dawkins, has thoroughly ingested the packaged profile of Jews, Judaism, and Hebrew Scripture passed down by the early church. Dawkins views it in company with many others: "The God of the Old Testament is arguably the most unpleasant character in all fiction: jealous and proud of it; a petty, unjust, unforgiving control-freak; a vindictive, bloodthirsty ethnic cleanser; a misogynistic, homophobic, racist, infanticidal, genocidal, filicidal, pestilential, megalomaniacal, sadomasochistic, capriciously malevolent bully."[2]

There are many examples of such oft-repeated perceptions that, in point of fact, have become the very texture of a highly flawed and perniciously anti-Judaic perspective. One has only to contrast Shakespeare's *The Merchant of Venice* character, Shylock, i.e. the Jew, who demands his "just" pound of flesh from the Christian character, Portia, who gives the magnificent speech on "the quality of mercy." This characterization is just one example of the many representations of Jewish character and values that have contributed to a highly errant understanding of Judaism as embodying a strict unloving justice and Christian scripture as embodying love-filled compassion.

In truth this "quality of mercy" that Portia speaks of so eloquently in *The Merchant of Venice*, is copied from Hebrew Scriptures' idea of *rachmanut* the Hebrew word for pity, mercy, along with *hesed* meaning lovingkindness and then—coupled with the concept of *tsedek*, (justice). These form the very legal spine of Western civilization and are central to the Jewish understanding of Torah. It is possible to ascribe the misperception of the Torah as just a book of exacting laws to the Greek translation of the Bible known as the Septuagint. To quote Rabbi Abraham Joshua Heschel, "The translators of the Septuagint committed a fatal and momentous error when, for lack of a Greek equivalent, they rendered Torah with *nomos,* which means *law,* giving rise to a huge and chronic misconception of Judaism and supplying an effective weapon to those who sought to attack the teachings of Judaism."[3]

2

I have titled this work *The Voice of Sarah* in order to invoke and query the true nature of this voice that inheres both explicitly and implicitly in the text and *midrash.* ' Sarah comes across both in the Bible as well as the *midrash* as Abraham's full partner. She is also at times referred to as a prophet. Sarah was a spiritual leader teaching the women about God while Abraham taught the men. In a passage of Torah that is the subject of numerous *midrashim* (plural of *midrash*). Sarah asserts that Abraham must banish Hagar and Ishmael. When Abraham demurs, God admonishes Abraham to listen to Sarah's voice and do all that she says. God, in other words, knows that Sarah's vision is prophetic and her judgment wise. The *midrash* states that when Abraham moved to a new venue, he set up Sarah's tent first as she was the one who drew people toward her. There was a light, a cloud that emanated from her tent from Shabbat to Shabbat. *Midrashim* contend that this light/cloud is the cloud of the *Shekhinah,* God's divine presence that hovered above her tent because of her infinite capacity to care for and administer to guests even if they were strangers. "All the years that Sarah was alive, there was a cloud [of the *Shekhinah*] at the entrance of her tent ...the doors of the tent stood wide open...there was blessing in the dough of the bread...there was a light burning from one Shabbat eve to the next Shabbat eve."[4] Her infinite capacity to nurture comes across in another *midrash* that discusses an event at the feast that marked Isaac's weaning. It seemed that because of Sarah's age, there was doubt that the child was really of her body. In order to quiet the doubt, Sarah uncovered her breasts and such copious milk flowed that she was able to feed all the babies that were in attendance at that great event, thus dispelling the notion that Isaac was not hers and at the same time nurturing all the many infants that were present. The legend continues

---

' I will have a great deal more to say about what constitutes *midrash* as well as other books of sacred text in the next chapter. Suffice to say for the present time the *midrash* consists of a series of books that deal with legends, stories, homilies from around 400CE'

that all of the babies nurtured by Sarah became converted to the idea of the One God.

Perhaps the most salient example of Sarah's voice is its very absence in the Bible's depiction of the "Binding of Isaac." The *midrashim* tell us that Abraham deliberately lies to Sarah in the "Binding of Isaac" as he knew that she would dissuade him from carrying out the sacrificial mission even though God had commanded it. Her voice is the voice of relationship, here seen as a mother's love for her child. It is the voice that prizes relationship over "overarching commands" even if they come from God. What gives fuel to the Rabbinic interpretations regarding her absence is that the following *parshah* (the segment of the Torah that is read each week) is entitled, *Chaye Sarah* or "The Life of Sarah" when it in fact begins with her death. The *midrashim* explain Sarah's death as her response to the sacrifice that might have taken place. How could her husband, Abraham, have acceded to this request from God? After all, it was Abraham who argued so eloquently with God on behalf of Sodom and Gomorrah. How could her God have asked this sacrifice? This realization on the part of Sarah that the sacrifice almost took place led to the dissolution of her most profound connections and thus to her demise.

It is interesting to consider the question posed by some of the Rabbis as to why God never again speaks to Abraham directly after this incident. Perhaps because he did not question God as he did regarding the destruction of Sodom and Gomorrah? It is difficult to see why Abraham would argue passionately against the destruction of the two cities and not even utter a word when asked by God to sacrifice his beloved son.

On *Rosh HaShanah*, we blow the shofar, the ram's horn which is supposed to remind us that God stayed Abraham's slaughter of Isaac and provided him with the ram to be sacrificed in his stead. However, an alternative *midrash* on the specific sound of the some of the notes of the shofar, the *shevarim* or broken notes are also reminiscent of Sarah's cry on hearing the specifics of the "binding," the near slaying of her son. Thus, on one of the most holy days of the Hebrew calendar, the voice of Sarah, the voice of relationship is sounded.

The analysis that follows makes the case that inherent within Judaism is the idea that ethics are not solely based on reason, that transcendent moral principles are not universally applied in making moral decisions, and that the primacy of relationship is at the very core of ethical consideration. In other words, this book will argue that feminist ethics are constitutive of Judaism. In order to fully make the case for this assertion, this book will illuminate the multitude of attributes that are part of God, specifically the attributes that we are called to emulate those of care, mercy and justice.

An Overview of the Book

In Chapter 1, I delineate how it is that Jews study sacred text and, how these methods differ radically from Christian study. I demonstrate that there is no such thing as a fundamentalist reading of the Bible even among the most rigorously orthodox community. The Hebrew Bible is never read by itself, but is read along with a vast commentary stemming over the course of almost two thousand years.

Chapter 2 discusses Object-Relations Theory, Care Ethics and Neuroscience. Here these modern terms are defined, explained and their relevance to feminism is delineated. The works of Carol Gilligan, Margaret Mahler, Nancy Chodorow, and others will be discussed in greater detail. This chapter discusses neuroscience in so far as it gives evidence to and validates the object-relations approach. Specifically it is the work of the object-relations theorists, since validated by modern neuroscience, which speaks to the concept of the self as relationally determined. How and why both the theories and the scientific evidence are relevant to Judaism and the study of sacred text will be explicated in subsequent chapters.

Chapter 3 discusses the "feminist" assumptions both implicitly and explicitly delineated within Jewish sacred text. The chapter examines the concept of *ona'at devarim*. The words basically refer to abusive or hurtful speech but can also be used when a person responds to another in need in a way that shows almost complete disregard or vast inability to empathize.

I reserve special emphasis for *hesed* often translated as loving-kindness as this is precisely the term most often omitted by those scholars, like Dawkins, for whom the concept fails to fit into their frameworks. Even though *hesed* is first used in text with relation to the patriarch, Abraham, it is through the female characters that *hesed* is most often either explicitly or implicitly manifested. Examples abound and will be singled out for discussion.

Chapter 4 discusses the word most often used in text to discuss justice, *tsedek*. The correct translation should be "righteousness." The question of whether this concept can be construed similarly to Western notions of what constitutes justice will be addressed. Specifically, the assertion to be pursued is that the word *tsedek* incorporates a relational perspective. I build on this treatment to discuss other words for justice, such as *din* and *mishpat* along with the word for compassion, *rahamim*. Instructively, this word derives from the word, *rehem* or womb.

Chapter 5 discusses the question of autonomy within a relational concept of the self. Questions of ethics, of individual responsibility, have been based on the idea of an individual acting autonomously.

Autonomy has in the psychology literature, notably in Freud and in Erikson, to be a hallmark of mental health. The trajectory of autonomy from their perspective starts when the child successfully separates, i.e. develops a sense of self as a separate entity from the mother, starting at around age 3. 18th century philosopher, Immanuel Kant defines autonomy as being the property of an individual rational self-conceived as a "self-contained unit," thus again seeing the self as totally separate. This book, on the contrary, defines the self as being constituted by relationships. How can we then look to the question of individual autonomy within the context of a relational self? This chapter presents some answers.

Chapter 6 will summarize and lead to the conclusion. The life, the character and the leadership of Moses will illustrate psychological concepts of "secure attachment" and again look to object relations theory to illuminate how empathy is inculcated and permeates the Jewish and feminist underpinnings of care, justice, and mercy.

The specific unique and traditional way Jewish text is studied, i.e. *hevruta* or, the study of a portion of text in pairs, is shown to enhance and augment the abilities of the partners to imbibe both the explicit and implicit moral dimensions of the text.

Chapter 7 concludes the book with a summation of the major tenets presented in the work along with some additional examples.

Endnotes: Introduction

[1] Joseph Campbell, "The Power of Myth," 1988 TV series with correspondent Bill Moyers.

[2] Richard Dawkins, *The God Delusion*, London: Transworld Publishers, 2007.

[3] Abraham Joshua Heschel, *God in Search of Man, A Philosophy of Judaism,* New York: Farrar, Straus, Giroux, 1955.

[4] *Midrash Bereshit Rabbah*, 60:10.

Chapter 1

How Jews Study Text

"This method (listening, reading, and interpreting text in a community) dictates that human life is essential, that human flourishing is rooted not simply in justice, but in love and mutuality and that righteousness (tsedek) and lovingkindness (hesed) are at the heart of human survival."[1]

The Judaic study of sacred text differs from how the Christian world studies its texts. Some Christian sects study the Bible as literal truth. Other sects, look to canonical writings of the early Church fathers such as Augustine and Aquinas as well as revered Protestant theologians such as Luther and Calvin for interpretations. Modern progressive pastors may use Christian feminist or liberation theology to augment interpretations based on these historical traditional readings[2] However, while text study is an important part of the religious enterprise, again, depending on the sect, most Christians prioritize faith, prayer, and good deeds. It can be stated that the absolute central religious activity of Judaism is textual study. Fundamental and unique to Jewish study of sacred text is that every textual line, or even every word is read with a plethora of many elements: linguistic associative connections, laws, stories that range from those of the second century BCE to contemporary time. These are nuanced and multilayered readings, some seemingly contradictory, which coexist in a tension that is inherently creative and demand constant interaction and reinterpretation. This textual reading never gives rise to a limited binary view. Matter and spirit, intellect and emotion, mind and body, immanence and transcendence, male and female, self and other, care and justice do not exist in a co-annihilating opposition but are constantly woven together in a unique whole. The very language used as well as the spaces in the text are replete with layers of meaning that become grist for the interpreter's mill. In Jewish textual analysis meaning is not fixed and there is no one truth. Investigation takes place usually within the context of a *hevrutah* study whereby two study partners seek to uncover meaning via argumentation, disputation, and debate.˙ Looking at Rabbinic˙˙ interpretations from ancient times, from medieval to modern commentary from the specifics of the text, always extrapolating to modern instances and then ever circling back to the words in the text themselves, the interpreters seek to augment, to add new examples to come up with additional insights which will then give rise to new arguments in an ever increasing and expanding web of interpretation and ambiguity that in some ways reflects and reconceives our world.

Professor Susan Handelman notes in her seminal book, *The Slayers of Moses,* that Christian tradition became "deeply embedded in Greek thought."[3] For the ancient Greeks, namely Plato and Aristotle, words are imperfect representations of some higher reality. Thus, the spiritual goal stemming from Greek thought and then passed down to Christian theology was to bring what is truly real "above" down here "below." For the Rabbis the Hebrew word, *dvar* means "thing" as well as "word." Writing of this distinction between the Christian and Judaic approaches, Susan Handelman notes: "Words create, characterize and

---

˙ I will have much more to say in Chapter 6 about how this method is itself an expression of the relational ethic that is at the heart of Judaism.

˙˙ The Rabbis or Rabbinic interpretation refers to the rabbis who interpreted, codified, developed, and augmented the Biblical text resulting in *Talmud, Midrash,* and other commentaries (from about 70CE to 1000CE).

sustain reality. The primary reality is linguistic. Thus, for Jews the central act is not incarnation but interpretation. Jewish spirituality begins and finally ends with the words of scripture. For the Rabbis the primary reality was linguistic. True being was a God who speaks and creates texts and "imitato deus" was not silent suffering but speaking and interpreting."[4]

As a prime example of Jewish textual analysis, we can begin at the beginning with Rashi's* comment on the very first words of Genesis, of *B'reshet,* "This passage calls for a *Midrashic* interpretation." He then goes on to aver the mystery that is present from "the beginning" in that using the syntax of the word *breshet* one translates the verse as "in the beginning of God's creation of heaven and earth." Rashi then admonishes us that if you take the verse to give you a chronology of the order of things, "you should be astonished at yourself for indeed the waters came first, for it is written 'and the spirit of God hovered over the face of the waters.'" He asks then, when did the creation of the waters take place? Torah scholar Avivah Zornberg observes, "What emerges from Rashi's provocative statements is a sense of the gaps, the unexplained, the *need to examine and reexamine* the apparently lucid text, with its account of a harmonious coherent cosmology."[5]

A second example comes from one of the most famous stories of all Rabbinic Judaism (and one that is so often misinterpreted) which goes as follows: It happened that a certain heathen came before Shammai (first century CE Jewish scholar whose views are often contrasted with Hillel's) and said to him, "convert me on condition that you teach me the entire Torah while I am standing on one foot." Shammai drove him away with the builder's measuring stick that was in his hand. The heathen then came before Hillel who converted him. Hillel said to him, "That which is hateful to you, do not do to your neighbor. This is the entire Torah; the rest is commentary—go and learn it."[6] The fact that

---

* Rashi is an acronym for Rabbi Schlomo Yitzhaki, 11th century Torah sage.

the "rest is commentary" seems at face value to be of little consequence. However, the antithesis is true. The "go study" admonition is to be taken very seriously. The admonition from Hillel to "go and study" implies the active engagement with all aspects of text.

The Sacred Texts

The central text of Judaism is Torah. Simply, that means the five books of Moses (Genesis, Exodus, Leviticus, Numbers and Deuteronomy). However, on another more extensive and deeper level, Torah is part of the *Tanakh,* the Hebrew Bible consisting of Torah, Prophets, and the remainder of the Canonical writings. (Judges, Kings, et al.) Torah, more commonly, also stands for much more than one book or one text. Torah encompasses the entirety of Jewish study down through the generations or what was known as the "oral Torah," with the tradition being that these commentaries were also given by God on Mt. Sinai orally as opposed to the revelation that was written Torah that God handed to Moses on Mt. Sinai. Torah can also refer to the sacred writings including *Mishneh, Talmud, Aggadah,* and medieval and modern commentary. These commentaries also include mystical tradition that is part of *Kabbalah.* Scholar Barry Holtz in *Back to the Sources* likens the structure of the sacred texts to an inverted pyramid. "The Bible is at the base, but the edifice expands outward enormously—*midrashic* literature, the *Talmuds*, the commentaries, the legal codes, the mystical tradition, the philosophical books. All this literature is Torah.[7] Again, what is essential to comprehend is that every word, every line in the original Biblical text is now surrounded by interpretive commentary in the form of law, parable, and homiletics. This study of Jewish texts, Torah, is what the sage Hillel meant when he told the potential convert to "go and study."

Because of the nature of Judaic study, it is important to delineate and define the various texts, terms, and concepts that constitute it.

Talmud usually refers to the rabbinic texts concerning religious and civil law derived from the Biblical text. *Midrash* (derived from the root "to search out") is the appellation for the totality of commentary (often referred to as *aggadah*) that involves narrative, parables, homilies, ethical and theological statements.* Biblical text is extremely laconic. *Midrash* is there to fill in the blanks, to tell us what is going on in the minds and hearts of the characters. The Hebrew word *pardes,* which literally means "orchard," is used in the study of Jewish sacred text and an acronymic guide toward layered interpretation. The "p" stands for the *pshat* or the simple, direct meaning, the "r" for the *remez* or the hints of meaning just beyond the literal text, the "d" for the *drosh* or *midrashic* interpretations that link the previous explanations with comparable passages throughout the Bible, and the "s", for the *sod* or the secret or mystical meaning of the textual passage.

Thus, as is clearly evident, there can never be an analog in Jewish study to a Christian fundamentalist reading of Biblical text. Another vital concept that must be emphasized here is that opposing points both in *Talmud* and in *Aggadah* are equally studied as sacred. These opposing views of a particular passage or segment are both listed on the page of *Talmud.* The particular passage is placed in the center of the page, the Rabbinic interpretations are placed all around the sides. Never mind that the opposition can be from different eras, if the sage is held in high esteem, the seeming dialog from across time spans is studied. The following quote refers to the fact that contrasting opinions from revered sages are both deemed holy. "Both these and these are utterances of the Living God."[8] Debate, according to famed Hasidic sage, Rabbi Nachman of Bratslav, is a holy form of communication. Debate is an echo of the divine process of *tzimtzum,* (God's self-limitation) making space for the creation of something new. "When we disagree with one another, when

---

* The dichotomy between *Halacha* or law that is elucidated in *Talmud and Aggadah*, the stories is never really clear cut. There are also homiletic stories that are part of Talmud.

13

we take sides, we create the necessary space for the emergence of new and unexpected ideas"[9] Thus debate becomes a holy act. What is striking about Judaism is that argument and the airing of contrary views is the essence of the religious life.[10]

In order to show that Jewish sacred text is commensurate with a psychological perspective on the nature of the self, specifically that of object-relations theory of a self that is "self-in-relation" and hence on the nature of the ethical, I must here change course. In this next chapter I will discuss in some detail object-relations theory and the recent validating work in neuroscience. Out of the dynamics of early identifications with the mother, empathic identifications achieved through secure attachment, extend beyond the mother to others. The self as defined by object-relations theory is developed as a subject that is able to take a position in the world as well as an entity that is constantly defined by its inter-subjective relationships with others. What emerges developmentally from these relationships is thus the motivation to repair whatever damage one has inflicted on the connection. This concept of repair is manifested throughout Jewish sacred text. It concerns personal relationships and extends to the entire world via the concept of *tikkun olam,* repairing the world. Taking responsibility for the well-being of others as a code of behavior is the very essence of an "ethic of care" which I argue is foundational to Jewish sacred text. Self-in-relation is an embodied phenomenon not just a psychological one. Therefore the recent work in neuroscience will be addressed in the next chapter as well.

Endnotes: Chapter 1

---

[1] Laurie Zoloth *Health Care and the Ethics of Encounter,* Chapel Hill: University of North Carolina Press, 2002.

[2] http://www.christianbiblereference.org/study_HowTo.htm).
http://www.wvdiocese.org/pages/pdfs/oldthingsmadenew/Chapter6.pdf.
Personal communication with Reverend Elaine Thomas, rector of All Saints Episcopal Church, Hoboken, New Jersey.

[3] Susan Handelman, *The Slayers of Moses*, Albany: SUNY Press, 1983, p.4.

[4] Ibid.

[5] Avivah Gottlieb Zornberg, *The Beginning of Desire: Reflections on Genesis,* Philadelphia: Jewish Publication Society, 1995 P. 6.

[6] Babylonian Talmud; Shabbat 31a quoted in Barry Holtz, *Back to the Sources,* New York Summit Books, 1984 p. 11.

[7] ibid. p. 13.

[8] Babylonian *Talmud,B. Eruvin.*13b).

[9] Rabbi Or Rose quoted in *Judaism's Great Debates,* Rabbi Barry Schwartz, Philadelphia: Jewish Publication Society.2012 p. xiii.

[10] Rabbi Lord Jonathan Sacks, modern Biblical scholar, former chief rabbi of Great Britain, has a weekly an on-line commentary on the week's *parshah.*

Chapter 2

Object Relations Theory, Neuroscience and Care Ethics

"It is not good for man to be alone."[1]

Expressed throughout this work is my assertion that Jewish sacred text as delineated in both law and in narrative extols and exalts the primacy of relationship. Implicit in the texts are concepts of "self-other" connection that in our current time would be labeled as feminist as this voice was re-discovered through the work of psychologist Carol Gilligan as she listened to girls and women. This voice is what I have called the "voice of Sarah." What follows in this chapter is a review of psychoanalytic object-relations theory and neuroscience that has refocused traditional Western thinking on the nature of the self, self-other relationships, and moral thinking. In following chapters I will give examples of how Jewish sacred text anticipates many of the views put forward by these above-mentioned theorists.

The concept of self as emerging from and constituted by relationship was originally put forward by a group of psychoanalysts, British and American, who deviated from traditional Freudian psychoanalytic theory because they placed their emphasis on the role of vital parent-child early relationships rather than on the role of instinct in formulating the nature of the self. These alternative theorists conceived of libido, which was originally defined by Freud as the energy of the sexual instinct, as object-seeking energy. From the moment of birth we look to form relationships with the "significant other" instead of using them for self-gratification as was alleged by Freud. But what at birth is just an innate mechanism to seek relationship soon becomes the very essence of the self and the foundation of its emergence as a relational entity. The self is to be understood first and foremost as always existing and defined in terms of very early primal relationships, and second in terms of any other relationship thereafter. All object-relations theories assert that the psychological and physiological aspects of the primal relationships contribute to the constitution of the self, although different theorists emphasized one aspect more than the other.

Ronald Fairbairn (1889-1964), one of the first and most well-known of these theorists to articulate the object-relations perspective viewed people "as being object-related by their very nature." For him, the fundamental unit of consideration was that of a self in relation to an "other" and the nature of the relationship in between. The self therefore is to be understood as always existing and defined by the terms of the relationships it has, remembers, desires or creates. "In the relational /structure model of Fairbairn, the shape of the self grows and changes from its experience in relationships, while at the same time the nature of the relationships it has are being shaped and changed by that self."[2]

For Kleinians˙ the rudimentary ego exists as a separate entity operating at first in a mechanistic way but emerges as the essence of the self through relationship with the mother. Her theory posits that the infant's internal world is built up through the simultaneous processes of introjection and projection of aspects of self and other. Elements of the self are projected into the objects and elements of the object are taken into the self (introjections). The mind operates in this manner in order to fight the battle between the forces of life and the forces of death, i.e. the

---

˙ Melanie Klein British Psychoanalyst (1882-1960).

fight between good and evil.* As a primary defense against the dread of death, both the self and the object are split into good and bad elements which can be projected and introjected. When the care of the mother is mainly experienced as pleasurable and is internally represented as "good" identification with the internal object can develop. Enhanced by cognitive growth the mind is able to integrate the fragmented elements of the self and of the objects into whole entities and acknowledge that good and bad lies in the self as well as in the other.[3]

For Donald Winnicott (1896-1971) the self is the result of representations of the very concrete relationship with the "other" more specifically with the mother. (He has said there is no baby without the mother and no mother without the baby.) Winnicott was first and foremost a pediatrician who observed the relationship between real mothers and their babies. He coined the term "good enough mothering" to denote that perfect attunement between mother and baby does not exist but there is a necessary amount of what we might call empathic care, what he called "the holding environment" that facilitates the healthy development of self. We can say that the self is empty space until furnished by identifications. A key aspect of the mother's role is to mirror or reflect back the child's own being, thereby facilitating the development of an authentic sense of self.

Despite these differences, object-relations theorists agree that early objects, the name given to significant other people by Freud, and the infant's relationship with them become internalized in the unconscious of the individual where they persist into adulthood affecting all aspects of the person's habits, expectations, views, and behaviors. Early positive object relations give rise to a self-determined subject that recognizes itself as the source of its mental activities and behavior (and now can assume

---

* It is to be noted that Klein's theory is analogous to Jewish ideas regarding the self as containing both the *yetzer ha'ra,* the evil inclination and the *yetzer ha'tov,* the good inclination.

responsibility for the consequences of its actions). Although self-determination is an important individual achievement, it is not enough, since the very essence of the self, its constituents, as conceived by object-relations theory, remains hidden despite all the complexity and sophistication of its adult manifestations. It is therefore imperative that we as individuals become aware of that very essence. People learn about themselves by knowing how they see and relate to the other people in their lives and how they in turn represent themselves in relations with these others. The ongoing process of realization that self and other constitute subjectivity allows for empathy to emerge. Moreover, the insight that a person is his/her relations with other people in life can in principle be generalized from relations to the personalized other to the idea that one is in relation to "any" other. The manifestation of the idea of the relational self is the ethics of care.

Research into brain development from modern neuroscience validates what object-relations psychologists have articulated. The momentous discovery in the 1980s of the "mirror neuron" system by Italian researchers has increased the amount of neurological material that augments and backs up the work of object-relations theorists. The mirror neuron system consists of a small circuit of cells in the premotor cortex and the inferior parietal cortex. Research has shown that these neuronal pathways fire in us when we observe others performing tasks and also when we observe others showing emotions. Thus our neuronal activity actually mirrors the activity that is happening in the brain of the ones performing the tasks and showing the emotions. It is further hypothesized that the mirror neuron system develops in early infancy through the interactions of parent and child. "If mirror neurons are actually shaped in our brain by the coordinated activities of mother and father and baby, then these cells not only embody [or reflect?] both self and other, but start doing so at a time when the baby has more of an undifferentiated sense of "us" than any sense of an independent "self," before the baby can pass the mirror recognition˙ test."[4] Marco Iacoboni goes on to explain that the firing rates of these mirror neuron cells is different for actions of the self and for actions of others. The rate for actions of the self is much much stronger than for those of others. "Thus mirror neurons embody both the interdependence of the self and other—by firing for the actions of both—and the independence we simultaneously feel and require, by firing more powerfully for actions of the self."[5] From the primary "us," however, the baby slowly but surely comes to perceive the other naturally and directly. Thus, as object-relations theorists observed, the sense of self emerges in relation to others.

The brain is malleable throughout our lifetimes. It had been thought that the brain was relatively fixed at birth with just a short critical period in early childhood where change, i.e. new connections could form. We now know how wrong this idea was. By the later half of the twentieth century, new research showed that many aspects of the brain can be altered even through adulthood. However, it is most plastic in infancy and early childhood. Nurture writes on nature, i.e. our genetic endowment is modified through the processes of both maturation and experience. A human being is born with approximately 100 billion neurons, and 50 trillion connections. What changes the brain in the first year of life is the growth of new connections due to experience. By the end of the first year neural connectivity consists of about 1,000 trillion synapses. The most important experience of an infant human being is its interaction with its mother, what is called the process of "attachment." Attachment is defined by the primary researchers in the field, John Bowlby and Mary Ainsworth, as "a deep and enduring emotional bond that connects one person to another across time and space."[6] Attachment is characterized by specific behaviors in children, such as seeking

---

˙ The mirror recognition test is administered by placing a red mark on the forehead of the baby usually about 18 months of age. The baby looks in the mirror and if s/he realizes that the image is of him/herself, i.e. points to his/her own forehead, the baby has passed the recognition test.

proximity with the attachment figure when upset or threatened. [7] Attachment behavior in adults toward the child includes responding sensitively and appropriately to the child's needs. Work on attachment can be seen from an object-relations view as its observational /experimental direct manifestation. Bowlby and Ainsworth claimed and then conducted empirical work which demonstrated that secure attachment between a child and parent is essential for later healthy relationships as well as profoundly affects emotional social, cognitive, and moral development. Secure attachment lays the groundwork for healthy development that includes being open, attuned to others, empathetic, and caring. Ainsworth found that what allows secure attachment to emerge is the attentive care of the mother. Secure attachment is at the very core of forming a secure sense of self from which comes the ability to explore to develop that sense of "I" while being attuned to the "we." Numerous studies in neurobiology and psychology give ample evidence to back up these assertions. It has been shown that attachment failure[8] results in impairments in the right brain's stress coping systems that lead to pathological manifestations throughout life. In secure attachments links between the reward, affiliation and stress management areas in the brain occur.* "Secure attachment facilitates right brain development, promotes efficient affect regulation, and fosters adaptive infant mental health."[9]

Care Ethics

When promulgating a moral theory that included women's voices in her 1982 groundbreaking work, *In a Different Voice*, Carol Gilligan used the object-relation theorists' view of the relational self as fundamental to her analysis of what she called "care ethics." She specifically called on the work of psychoanalyst, Nancy Chodorow [10] who had interpreted the

---

* Specifically in the striatum.

theoretical work of object-relations theorist Margaret Mahler˙ in light of gender differences in self-conception. Mahler had delineated a stage theory of self-development where at birth, the child and mother are fused in the child's mind and then the child slowly develops a sense of self separate from the mother through the processes of separation and individuation when the "good-enough" mother (as per Winnicott) becomes internalized. Separation-individuation involves several sub-stages in which the child navigates a type of "dance" between seeking separateness and yet returning to make sure the mother is still there. As the mother-child relationship becomes securely internalized the child can then emerge as a separate yet internally connected individual. As stated above, Chodorow further elucidated Mahler's stages by looking at gender differences in the development of self. According to Chodorow,[11] girls retain the permeability of boundaries between self and other because issues of self are related to identifications with what is similar between girls and mother especially the femaleness that the mother represents. Boys' selves are developed as separate from those of their mothers because of the oppositional nature of perceived masculinity and the feminine, which the mother embodies. Thus, the original empathic tie becomes severed in boys in order to achieve "masculinity" especially when the larger culture defines masculinity in opposition to femininity. The disparate male and female perspectives on the world and people in it stem directly from differences in the nature of the self as separate versus self-in-relation. Thus Gilligan's work on notions of what constitutes the "ethical" highlighted disparate moral orientations between genders, where most women and girls do not see morality as based on fairness and (Western notions) of dispassionate justice as do most men, but rather on connection, care, emotion, and response. In the past the overwhelming consensus from both developmental psychology notably, Freud, Piaget, and Kohlberg, and moral philosophy, Plato, Aristotle, and Kant, was that advanced moral thinking and ethical decision making is based on

---

˙ Margaret Mahler (1897-1985).

overarching moral principles where specific cases are subsumed to these Kantian principles, i.e. Kant's "categorical imperative: "Act only on that maxim whereby you can at the same time will that it becomes a universal law."[12] These imperatives of the moral worth of an action are based on its inherent content rather than its effect.˙ If the judged ethical worth of an action must be based on principles that transcend specific situations then women, as Gilligan pointed out, have a problem. For example, if it is deemed by dint of a Kantian categorical imperative that killing is wrong even when the person is suffering and in great pain and is asking for death, then to commit this mercy killing is judged as morally wrong. However, if the person doing the killing is helping a loved one and wishes to alleviate unmitigated suffering then it is the specific situation and the specific relationship that determines the moral worth not the transcendent principle. The so-called murderer is so moved and feels that pain of the loved–one that it is impossible to not act. The fact is that these types of decisions have been deemed as less worthy than decisions based on Kantian ideals. It was alleged in a very disparaging way that women's morality was tied up in emotions and relationships. Gilligan found in her studies that girls and women often based moral decisions on specific situations and that these decisions, are based on care, and often involved compromise rather than taking an absolutist stance. At the same time, existing Western cultural narratives disparaged women's morality as tied up in emotions and relationships. (Freud, Piaget, Kohlberg) Gilligan quotes Freud as observing, "Women's superego (moral agency) was never so inexorable, so impersonal, so independent of its emotional origins as we require it to be in men. Women show less sense of justice than men, that they are less ready to submit to the great exigencies of life, that they are more often influenced in their judgments by feelings of affection or hostility."[13]

Gilligan's initial work has led to a paradigm shift in that "care ethics" has become more mainstream in philosophy and specifically in

---

˙ Antithetical to Jewish conceptions where moral worth is judged by action.

ethics. Recent work, specifically by moral philosopher Michael Slote, has emphasized the idea of empathy as underlying both care and justice. Empathy involves emotion and a sense of self that remains interconnected. Moral principles can in this model stem originally from empathic ties to personal others (the connected-self) and then through increasing cognitive understanding and complexity become the basis for these principles.[14]

Work from neuroscience has provided significant empirical support to work in philosophy and ethics. Antonio Damasio* and others have observed the relationship between emotion and reason that "emotions organize—rather than disrupt--rational thinking...emotions guide our perceptions of the world, our memories of the past and even our moral judgments of right and wrong"[15] As previously discussed, the discovery of "mirror neurons" provides further validity to the notion that the self-arises from relationship, from emotional connections between caregiver and infant.

As stated, if we look to male development, difference is the point of departure; the male separates from the mother in a more emphatic way and the mother sees the male as "other" and encourages the separation. What results in terms of moral decision making especially if enhanced by cultural norms around masculinity is a morality based on logic and reason. When similarity to the mother is emphasized as with the girl, then decision-making is based on emotion and care. We have learned through object-relations theory that neither the boy nor the girl is who they are without the mother. As healthy development proceeds psychic integration is achieved and both emotion and reason are combined to make moral decisions. The larger culture can then exert its influence often through the stories and the myths it tells. Do they value concrete human relationships or extol total independence? Jewish foundational

---

* Antonio Damasio, (b.1944) noted neuroscientist. Of particular note for this work are two of his books: *Descartes Error* (1994) and *The Feeling of What Happens* (1999).

stories are of families, of relationships, of caring for the stranger. One should not forget that Jewish laws of care are practices that were generalized from concrete relationships; they are the extension of the practice of care of the mother to the neighbor, city member, and beyond. Let's also not forget that these laws of care were conceived in the mind of generations of men in a process of interpretations. In order to formulate such laws these men had to become connected with their emotions. In order for this meaningful emotional connection to take place, psychological connection to the mother, had to be restored.

If one were to extrapolate from the works of Carol Gilligan and others who advocate for an ethic of care, on what would constitute feminist jurisprudence, one could say that it would consist of a system that would emphasize the repair of relationships rather than rules and precedents, look to the context of each specific situation rather than a rule applicable in all cases. There would be more emphasis placed on mediation and less on assigning damages. The case to be articulated here is that feminist ethics is integral to Jewish concepts of justice, law, care, and mercy, centuries before this concept was even presented. It is my contention that implicit in all the concepts to be elucidated is the traditionally non-Western, i.e. non-Cartesian˙ idea is that the self is constituted by its relationships to others, to the world, and to God. Interdependence characterizes the nature of self (self-in-relation) and forms the underpinnings of that which characterizes Jewish concepts of justice, care, and mercy. Again, these concepts have to be contrasted with previous Western notions that have highlighted the self as separate, rational, individual.[16]

The above assertions regarding Jewish law and primacy of relationships will be discussed and illuminated by examples in the upcoming chapters.

˙ Rene Descares a 17th century French philosopher known for his dualistic theory of the mind-body problem; specifically his belief that the essence of the mind was thinking.

Endnotes: Chapter 2

[1] *Jewish Publication Society Hebrew-English Tanakh:* Gen; 2:18.

[2] Richard Rubens, "Fairbairn's Structural Theory",
http://www.columbia.edu/%7Err322/FAIRBAIRN.html.

[3] Elizabeth Spillius, *Melanie Klein Today: Developments in Theory and Practice,* vol. 1, London and New York: Routledge, New Library of Psychoanalysis, 1988.

[4] Marco Iacoboni, *Mirroring People: The New Science of How We Connect with Others,* New York: Farrar, Strauss, and Giroux, 2008. p155.

[5] Ibid.

[6] John Bowlby, *Attachment and Loss,* Vol. 1, New York: Basic Books, 1969. Mary Ainsworth, "The Development of Infant-Mother Attachment", in *Review of Child Development Research,* Bettye Cardwell and Henry Ricciuti, eds., Chicago: University of Chicago Press, 1973.

[7] Bowlby, op.cit.

[8] Allen Schore, "The Effect of Early Relational Trauma on Brain Development, Affect Regulation and Infant Mental Health"
http://onlinelibrary.wiley.com/doi/10.1002/1097-
0355(200101/04)22:1%3C201::AID-IMHJ8%3E3.0.CO;2-
9/abstract;jsessionid=A49C828802B11A73B67B391B844E22C4.f03t01.

[9] Ibid.

[10] Nancy Chodorow, *The Reproduction of Mothering: Psychoanalysis and the Sociology of Gender,* Berkeley: University of California Press, 1978.

[11] Ibid.

[12] Immanuel Kant, https://plato.stanford.edu/entries/kant-moral/

[13] Sigmund Freud cited by Carol Gilligan, *In a Different Voice,* Cambridge: Harvard University Press 1982.

[14] Michael Slote, *The Ethics of Care and Empathy,* London and New York: Routledge, 2007.

[15] Keltner Dacher and Paul Ekman,"The Science of Inside-Out" New York Times, 7/5/2015.

[16] Steven Friedell, "The Different Voice in Jewish Law," *Indiana Law Journal,* vol. 67, 1992.

Chapter 3

The Feminine-Relationship-Interdependence

We are, as Gilligan stressed, constituted by relationship. Moral decisions are often based in emotion and are considered within the context of a caring relationship. The texts of Judaism stress this notion of the sacredness of such relationships. Even God needs relationship with humanity according to Rabbi A. J. Heschel[1] who stated God seeks relationship with human beings. God is not God without response from human beings. Heschel continues that "God is not Aristotle's 'unmoved mover' but on the contrary, He is the most moved mover." Rabbi Yael Splansky˙ in a recent *d'var Torah* (commentary on the weekly Torah reading) quotes from Rabbi David Hartman, "In secular life, independence may be the sought after mark of strength, but in Judaism, healthy interdependence is the ideal. God is diminished not in power but in effectiveness when left alone. God needs a partner. We are God's witnesses." Splansky continues her discussion by citing rabbinic commentary on the verse, "you are My witnesses" she states that the Rabbis imagine God saying, "When you are My witnesses, I am God. When you are not My witnesses, it is as if I am not God."[2] Splansky goes on to say "Of course God was always God, but until Abraham came along and pointed and said, 'This is the one God of the universe,' it was as if God did not exist." The above cited line is reminiscent of the

---

˙ Contemporary rabbinical scholar based in Toronto, Canada.

question often posed by college students in an introductory psychology course. "If a tree falls in the forest, and there's no one around, does it make a sound?" The answer is "no," sound waves are generated but you need an experiencing organism with the appropriate sense receptors for a sound to be heard. God needs relationship with human beings in much the same way, requiring the experiencing human to be receptive to God.

The Primacy of Relationship

There are textual clues to the importance of this notion of receptivity in the Hebrew Bible. It is noteworthy, for example, that there is no word for, no counterpart to the English word "obey." The word used is *shema*, or "listen!" The first prayer that every Jewish child learns is "*Shema Yisrael, Adnonai Elohanu, Adonai echad*" which translates to "Hear Israel, the Lord your God, the Lord is one." We are asked to listen to God's voice, called to enter into relationship, into covenant.

According to Rabbi Jonathan Sacks,˙ in a *d'var Torah* on *Parshat Yitro*, the Hebrew word for life *chayyim* is plural as if to signify that life is essentially shared. Rabbi Sacks continues that Dean Inge (a noted Anglican theologian) once defined religion as "what an individual does with his own solitude". That is not a Jewish thought.

Prime examples where care and relationship assert primacy over disembodied reason come from a number of *Talmudic* discussions about where and how violence accompanies the severing of relationship. Most of the Rabbis taught that a man studying abroad for extended periods should return home at least once per week. (Shabbat) to be with his wife (sexually). What occurs if the stay is longer is that tragedy befalls the scholar. The story of Rav Rehumi illustrates this principle: he absented himself from his wife for a year and would return home every Yom

---

˙ Rabbi Lord Jonathan Sacks (b.1948) former chief rabbi of the United Kingdom, noted contemporary Torah scholar and philosopher.

Kippur. "On one occasion his learning attracted him and he did not return home. His wife was expecting him every moment saying: He is coming soon, he is coming soon. But he did not come. She became so depressed that tears began to flow from her eyes. He was at that moment sitting on a roof. The roof collapsed under him and he was killed" According to the Rabbis, in the end her tears kill him. Rav Rehumi did not have the ability to truly understand his wife's pain and for that he was punished severely.[3]

There is another Talmudic story that bears mentioning here, referred to as *The Oven of Akhnai.* I will have much more to say on this particular story in a later chapter. As the story goes, there is a dispute among the Rabbis as to whether or not an oven is clean. The majority rule one way, a single rabbi, Rabbi Eliezer, another. The majority wins the argument but then the majority retaliates against Rabbi Eliezer in such as way as to humiliate him. In fact they burn his work, strip him of his position, and cast him out from among his people.[4] What then ensues are a number of disasters, including withering crops and even the death of one of the sages, Rabban Gamliel. The take-away for present purposes is that severing the relationship is tantamount to bringing about disaster.

Ona'at Devarim

The interpersonal and relational nature of Jewish morality may be epitomized by the commandment of *ona'at devarim.* The translation is usually given as "verbal wronging." However, as Tova Hartman points out in her book *Are You Not a Man of God?* the term has been augmented to encompass situations where other's feelings are not comprehended sufficiently where the subjective experience of hurt is held as an extreme example of wrongdoing on the part of one who should know better.

The story of Hannah in the Bible gives Hartman the ammunition she needs to emphasize the importance of *ona'at devarim*. Hannah, distraught by her inability to have children, prays silently, pouring out her heart to God at the sanctuary at Shiloh. Only her lips move. Eli, the high priest, observes her behavior and jumps to the erroneous conclusion that she is drunk. He castigates her for her drunkenness. "How long will you make a drunken spectacle of yourself? Sober up"[5] As the Bible states in the book of Samuel, Hannah then rebukes Eli: "Did you not know that I am a woman of aggrieved spirit?" Hartman points out that in *midrash*, Hannah's reproach encompasses so much more. "You are not a master in this matter, and the Divine Spirit does not rest upon you, that you suspect me of this thing." Eli thus has compounded the hurt that Hannah feels by his insensitive misunderstanding and then his cursory response to her prayers. He thus loses all credibility despite his high position. He has committed *ona'at devarim*. According to the Rabbis, Hannah becomes the very model for prayer, as evidenced by the *amidah*, the silent prayer repeated multiple times during daily and Sabbath services. Hartman continues that the Rabbis in their discussion of *ona'at devarim* highlight the fact that it is especially pertinent to women. She writes that:

> This move holds the seeds of something radical: the subjective experience of women – what the Talmud associates with heightened interpersonal sensitivity, and a kind of emotionality that can be unpredictable even volatile-rather that being dismissed as "histrionic" or "hysterical' and understood as incompatible with the needs of normative legislation-is not only legitimated, but given a place of pride within a critical sphere of the law. The Rabbis give legal authority to this "female perspective, stamping the "care voice" with the imprimatur of the "justice voice" making the two so interdependent that the line between them is substantially blurred.[6]

We see an interesting counterpoint to the high priest in the Hannah story with the tale of the prophet Elisha and the Shumamite woman. After a time of being without child, the Shumamite woman gives birth to a son seemingly as a reward for having always made a place and cared for the prophet Elisha when he was in the vicinity. However, some years after the birth, the son sickens and it appears that he dies. The woman goes to find Elisha: "And when she came to the man of God to the hill, she caught hold of his feet. And Gehazi [Elisha's servant] came near to thrust her away; but the man of God said: 'Let her alone; for her soul is bitter within her; and the LORD hath hid it from me, and hath not told Me.'"[7] Thus as Elisha's servant is about to dismiss her, the prophet sees and recognizes her and feels her anguish. He then goes with the woman and revives the child. We can thus infer that Elisha truly embodies this capacity to empathize, to feel the pain of the woman and in Hartman's words, he is truly a "man of God."

Hesed

As I have argued elsewhere,[8] this work contends that the concept of "care" is nicely elucidated in Torah (understood in the all-inclusive sense as the entire body of Jewish sacred text as *hesed,* often translated as "loving-kindness." The post-medieval commentator, Rabbi Yehuda Loew of Prague (1575-1609), known as the *Maharal* (acronym in Hebrew for "our teacher the Rabbi Loew), as cited in Zornberg stated "*Mishpat,* absolute standards of justice, cannot be realized in this world as God has created it. To adhere to such standards is to destroy the world; in order to build the world, *hesed,* the generous perception of alternative possibilities is necessary."[9] *Gemilut hasadim,* performing acts of loving-kindness is said to be one of the pillars on which the world stands.[10]

According to Gordon Clark in his erudite work on the uses and meaning of the word *hesed* in the Hebrew Bible, "*hesed* is an attribute of God. It is rooted in divine nature and it is expressed because of who God is, not because of what humanity needs. God expects his people to emulate this quality that he so frequently demonstrates even though people's expression of it can only be a pale reflection of God's."[11] It is often through the female characters that *hesed* is most often either explicitly or implicitly manifested. For example Rebecca, the wife of Isaac, was found by Abraham's servant Eliezer among Abraham's extended family. The process by which she was found and vetted is depicted in the Biblical text. There the word *hesed*, loving-kindness, is used four times. Eliezer prays for guidance in his mission with the following: "Here, I have stationed myself by the water spring as the women of the two go out to draw water. May it be that the maiden to whom I say: Pray lower your pitcher that I may drink, and she says: Drink, and I will also give your camels to drink—let her be the one that you have decided on for your servant, for Isaac, by means of her may I know that you have dealt faithfully with my lord."[12] Rebecca comes to the well and proceeds to do exactly what Eliezer had hoped. Biblical and Near Eastern scholar Tikva Frymer-Kensky adds to Rebecca's deed by pointing out that "Ancient Near Eastern wells were not vertical shafts through which buckets are lowered by rope. They were inclined slopes that the girl went down and came up. To water ten camels after a long journey, Rebecca had to go down and come up many times."[13]

The following legend from the *midrash* is in regard to Shifra and Puah, the midwives who disobey Pharoah's order to kill Jewish male babies. According to Avivah Zornberg, the midwives not only birthed but nurtured and sustained life.[14] Louis Ginzberg, in his book, *Legends of the Jews*, writes that not only did the midwives not murder the babies but supplied all their wants and needs. They said to themselves "Our father Abraham opened an inn, that he might feed the wayfarers, though they were heathen, and we should neglect the children, nay kill them: No, we shall have a care to keep them alive."[15] In each of the examples the Biblical text, augmented by *midrashic* legends, highlight how care is held as an abiding ethic.[16] Facing death if discovered, the midwives not only continue to perform their job, but act heroically by providing for the babies' nurture. The legend about Abraham provides an example for the midwives but also reminds us that "care" was exemplified in Abraham's behavior towards all people. It is often noted that Abraham is the Biblical figure that most embodies *hesed* in his willingness to care for strangers, to attend to their needs. God in fact chooses Abraham as His favorite. (He did not choose Nimrod the first hero of the Bible*). "I have chosen him that he may charge his sons and his household after him to keep the way of the Lord, to do righteousness and justice."[17]

The concept was augmented in the *Tannaitic*** period and from the later *Talmudic* period with the elevation of the matriarchs and in particular with their relationship with God. "It is occupied with the question of who the matriarchs were and discusses how God was revealed in their lives, often by way of expressions of personal piety that are characterized as deeds of loving-kindness.[18] Einat Ramon in her article, "The Matriarchs and the Torah of *Hesed*," goes on to say that the Rabbis intended to emphasize the presence of God in the small details of the matriarchs' everyday lives.

"The *midrashim* express profound admiration of the matriarchs' ability to render the divine presence immanent in the running of the home and the evolution of the family."[19] We thus see that the Jewish concept of God include the transcendent and the immanent, the most-moved mover of Heschel. While the revelation at Sinai is the seminal event in Torah, the daily activities and experiences relating to loving-kindness are no less essential and are manifestations of the covenant between God and the people. Responsibility in the home is emphasized

---

* Nimrod is described in Gen. 10:8–12 as "the first on earth to be a mighty man. He was a mighty hunter before the Lord."
** Early Rabbinic interpretation from the 1st and 2nd centuries CE.

among these quotidian acts. Every adult is responsible for the rearing and teaching of children.

"It was a central and substantive claim of justice that everyday ethical relationships were the measure of the ethical claims of the entire system. Human life is essential and human flourishing is rooted not simply in justice, but in love and mutuality, and that righteousness and lovingkindness are at the heart of human survival."[20] To return to a further elucidation of the term *hesed* as manifested by *gemilut hasadim*, a passage in the *Tosefta,* defines *hesed* as being synonymous with acts of loving-kindness – according to Einat Ramon. Maimonides in his *Guide to the Perplexe*[21] defines *gemilut hasadim* as encompassing deeds of extraordinary kindness for which no limit has been prescribed. They include showing kindness to those who have no claim whatever upon us, and showing kindness above and beyond what is due to those to whom we owe some sort of legal recompense. These deeds have both an emotional and practical dimension as they transcend the legal and human obligations specified in the commandments.

Modern scholar Tikva Frymer-Kensky[22] poses the question in her book *Reading Women of the Bible*, how do women prophets differ from their male counterparts? She answers her own query by stating that the female prophets do not really castigate or reprove either kings or the people of Israel as that is not their calling but what they do is to convey the will of God, by "listening to deep inner voice, i.e. greater sense of self and connection to a wider sphere."[23]

Suzanne Last Stone, in her article "Justice, Mercy and Gender in Rabbinic Thought," cites a *midrash* (from *Eicha Rabbah*) where the three patriarchs and Moses try to dissuade God from continuing the punishment of Israel after the destruction of the temple and allow them to return. God is not persuaded by their legalistic arguments. It is Rachel's emotional pleading that triggers God's mercy. Rachel reminds

---

* Additional law and commentary from the 2nd century CE.

God that she gave Leah the signs that she and Jacob planned knowing that Laban would try to trick Jacob and that she, Rachel, had hid under her sister's marriage bed with Jacob in order not to shame her sister and to subdue her own jealousy to make sure her sister was not shamed. The word used in the text is *hesed*, i.e. that she Rachel had shown *hesed* toward her sister. It is Rachel's pleading that triggers God's mercy on behalf of the people, Israel.[24]

It needs to be emphasized again that the concept of *hesed* is most often part of both the Biblical and *midrashic* text associated with women although it is with Abraham that we first encounter this word. The concept of *hesed* reaches its height in the Book or Ruth. The Book of Ruth is known in rabbinic literature as *Torat Hesed*. In the *midrash*, Rav Zeira is cited as saying: "The *megillah* does not contain within it the laws of purity or impurity, the permissible or the impermissible. Then why was it written? To teach the great reward of those who show loving-kindness (*hesed*) to others. Ruth is a poor, relatively young widow who marries a Judean man, a woman whose *hesed* and maternity grant her a place in Israel's memory. Her claim to fame results from her actions in the domestic and familial spheres." [25] When refusing to abandon Naomi, Ruth embodies *hesed*, Ruth's loyalty to her mother-in-law inspires wealthy Boaz who extends generosity toward Ruth, stretching himself beyond the call of duty, one act of *hesed* inspires others. *Hesed* in Ruth is not so much a case of good people doing good things, but rather an example of how ordinary people with mixed motives become extraordinary through the cultivation of *hesed*. Although *hesed* in Ruth is explicitly ascribed to human beings, the text suggests that those who act with *hesed* mirror the ways of God, serving as agents of God's *hesed* through their deeds of kindness. In this text it is the *hesed* shown by Ruth that engenders the *hesed* shown by Boaz. Thus the woman here becomes the catalyst embodying God's *hesed*. "Megilat Ruth is a book about kindness (hesed) and audacity, about kindness that propels people to act audaciously for the sake of others."[26]

It is again worth highlighting that it is the interpersonal, the relational that is the very basis of the moral and ethical codes and is extolled in Judaic text. In this chapter we have seen it manifested directly in the mutual need of relationship between God and His people, in the concept of *ona'at devarim* and in the word *hesed.* The next chapter continues with a discussion of the significance and nuanced meanings of the words for "justice" and "pity."

Endnotes: Chapter 3

[1] Rabbi Abraham Joshua Heschel (1907-1972) formidable influential Jewish scholar. Much of the here referenced material comes from his book *God in Search of Man,* New York: Farrar, Straus, and Giroux, 1955.

[2] *Pskikta D'Rav Kahana,* cited by Splansky.

[3] Tova Hartman and Charlie Buckholtz, *Are You Not a Man of God,* Oxford: Oxford University Press, 2014, p.167.

[4] Ibid.

[5] Sam.1:11.

[6] Hartman, op.cit., p. 56.

[7] 2 Kings 4:27.

[8] Susan Schept, "Hesed: Feminist Ethics in Jewish Tradition" *Conservative Judaism,* Vol. 57, no, 1 Fall 2004.

[9] Cited in Avivah Gottlieb Zornberg, *The Beginning of Desire: Reflections on Genesis,* Philadelphia: Jewish Publication Society, 1995, p. 44.

[10] From *Pirkei Avot,* Ethics of the Fathers.

[11] Gordon R. Clark, "The Word Hesed in the Hebrew Bible," *Journal for the Study of the Old Testament,* 1993.

[12] Gen. 24:67.

[13] Tikva Frymer-Kensky, *Reading Women of the Bible,* New York: Schocken Books, 2002, p. 38.

[14] Zornberg, *op.* cit.

[15] Louis Ginzberg, *Legends of the Jews,* (7 volumes), Philadelphia: Jewish Publication Society, 1909.

[16] Schept, op.cit.

[17] Gen. 18:19.

[18] Einat Ramon, "*The Matriarchs and the Torah of Hesed,*" *Nashim* 10 Fall 2005, pp. 154-177.

[19] Ibid.

[20] Laurie Zoloth, *Health Care and the Ethics of Encounter: A Jewish Discussion of Social Justice,* Chapel Hill, University of North Carolina Press, 1999, 218.

[21] Ramon *op. cit.*

[22] Frymer-Kensky op. cit.

[23] Ibid.

[24] Suzanne Last Stone, "Justice, Mercy and Gender in Rabbinic Thought," *Law and Literature,* Vol 8, no. 1, 1996, pp. 139-177.

[25] The Jewish Publication Society Commentary on Ruth, XXVI.

[26] Ibid.

Chapter 4

Justice and Compassion

"Justice has widely been said to be the moral value, which singularly characterizes Judaism both conceptually and historically. Historically, the Jewish search for justice begins with Biblical statements like "Justice, justice shall ye pursue."* On the conceptual side, justice holds a central place in the Jewish world-view, and many other basic Jewish concepts revolve around the notion of justice."[1]

"And you shall do the right and the good in the eyes of the Lord"[2]

"This refers to compromise rather than judgment according to strict law and conduct beyond the requirements of the law"[3]

There are several words that the Hebrew Bible uses that are translated into English as "justice," including *tsedek, mishpat,* and *din.* They are found in different contexts. Their meanings are nuanced and defy very specific translations.

We can aver, however, that the relational meaning of justice is exemplified in the use of the word *tsedek.* It is used most often in Genesis and in Deuteronomy including in this chapter's epigraph from Deut.16:20. *Tsedek* actually should be translated as "righteousness." *Tsedek* translated as righteousness, according to author Jason Ripley is inherently "relational "involving the fulfillment of the demands of relationships" between human beings and between the individual and

---

* Deut. 16:20.

God. [4] Thus, in the context of judicial systems, *tsedek* defined as righteousness must be understood as demanding not impartial decisions purely based on an abstract legal norm but, rather, as protective and restorative actions that fulfill communal demands and repair the community by helping those who have had their rights taken from them by others. We can assert that restorative justice is manifest in Jewish concepts of "punishment." According to modern scholar Rabbi Jill Jacobs*, the goal of punishment is threefold: first is to lead the wrongdoer to *tshuvah,* repentance; second to see the person as still made in the image of God, and that once the punishment has taken place, this person again becomes a viable member of the community (in fact the word used is *achicha,* your brother); and third to cultivate a just society. This emphasis on social justice is the overwhelming refrain of nearly every prophet and is a repeated point in Wisdom literature (Job, Ecclesiastes, Song of Songs and especially Proverbs): "Do not defraud the widow the orphan, the stranger, and the poor; and do not plot evil against one another". [5] As the scholar Jon Levinson observes "Justice, specifically used in the word *tsedek,* is constituted by compassion, by special solicitude for the powerless and disadvantaged, a determination that they not be victimized. That determination is not peculiar to courts of law. The Hebrew Bible expects it of everyone." [6]

The *Encyclopedia Judaica*" states that "righteousness is not an abstract notion but rather consists in doing what is just and right in all relationships."

The justice of "righteousness" (*tsedek*) goes beyond the claims of strict justice One can even argue that abstract notions of disembodied justice or righteousness are not part of Torah. In point of fact, according

---

* Rabbi Jill Jacobs (b.1975), Executive Director of T'ruah: The Rabbinic Call for Human Rights.
" The Encyclopedia Judaica is a 26 volume encyclopedia of the Jewish people and of Judaism.

to modern day Torah scholar Rabbi Bradley Shavit Artson,* there are no laws in Torah that are immutable. As an example, he cites the ritual of the *sotah*. If a man accuses his wife of infidelity, she first has the right to divorce him. If she chooses to prove her innocence, she is bidden to drink a potion consisting of dust from the Temple floor, and a charcoal curse containing God's name, which is melted into the water potion. If her body swells, she's considered guilty. However, if nothing happens as is most likely since all she did was drink dirty water, she is innocent beyond any doubt. The issue here is that God allows his name to be erased, which is in most cases, considered to be a sin. One is not allowed to even say God's name, books containing God's name are never to be discarded but are ritually buried. According to the *midrash* "in the case of the Holy Name, inscribed in sanctity, Scripture orders that it is to be blotted out in water to bring about peace between a man and his wife."[7]

The authors of this part of the *Encyclopedia Judaica* also characterize the sense of justice as "substantive," i.e. what human life should be like. "The substantive view of justice is concerned with the full enhancement of human, and, above all, social life. Thus it suffuses all human relations and social institutions." The meaning of righteousness is broadened to include actions beyond the letter of the law in the realms of ethics and ritual[8].

Noah and *Tsedek*

Note that the word *tsedek* is used to describe Noah as righteous in his time. "These are the generations of Noah. Noah was in his generations a man righteous and whole-hearted; Noah walked with God."[9]

Noah's righteousness is illustrated in the *midrash* by his loving attention to his animals. When God was looking to find a righteous

---

* Rabbi Bradley Shavit Artson, Vice President of American Jewish University, Dean's Chair, Ziegler School of Rabbinic Studies.

individual to save before the onset of the deluge he was looking to find someone who manifested care. God chose Noah to survive the destruction of humankind and all other living things because of his ability to care. Noah's wisdom is demonstrated in his painstaking, detailed knowledge of the feeding schedules of every species with the ark. "For twelve months in the ark, he had not a wink of sleep, neither by day nor by night, for he was occupied in feeding the creatures who were with him."[10]

Tsedakah

> "Poverty is not natural. It is manmade, and it can be overcome and eradicated by the actions of human beings. And overcoming poverty is not a gesture of charity. It is an act of justice." — Nelson Mandela

The word that is often translated in English as "charity" is *tsedakah*. It is important to note that Hebrew words have most often a three letter root, sometimes it is two, from which many words are derived. Thus the root for *tsedek* (ts-de-k) is the basis for the word *tsedakah*, the root being the same. This word also should be translated as "righteousness" as it implies that justice is manifested in helping others. Importantly, when translated as righteousness rather than charity, *tsedakah* implies non-hierarchical relationship. Contrary to the common metaphor of stooping to give charity, denoting an economic and moral condescension through the analog of posture, *tsedakah* as righteousness reminds us that we are not to see ourselves as better than the one receiving what we offer.

Strict Justice and Going Beyond the Letter of the Law

When speaking of strict justice, the words *din* or *mishpat* are commonly used. However, these words are rarely used on their own without being paired with mercy (*rahamim*) or care (*hesed)* or both. These qualities

41

are never viewed in terms of one precluding the other but are held as part of a unique "whole" world-view. The Rabbis of the *midrash* "conceive of justice and mercy as two polarities of a paradoxically unified divine whole."[11]

Midrashim abound from the beginning of Genesis where the Rabbis muse as to what was taking place in God's mind when creating or even before creating the world. "Upon setting out to create the world, God thought: If I create the world through My attribute of mercy, then sinners will be plentiful; if I create the world through My attribute of justice, then how will the world endure? I will create the world with a mixture of both attributes and hope that it will be able to endure."[12] Another similar *midrash* observes "Nor is this world inhabited by man the first of the earthly created by God. He made several worlds before ours, but He destroyed them all because He was pleased with none until He created ours. But even this last world would have had no permanence, if God had executed His original plan of ruling it according to the principle of strict justice. It was only when He saw that justice by itself would undermine the world that He associated mercy with justice and made them to rule jointly."[13]

It is often the case that what is stressed by the Rabbis is the importance of going beyond the letter of the law, rather than adhering to its "strict" observance. When addressing the reasons for the Roman conquest of Jerusalem, including the destruction of the temple, questions were asked, "Why was Jerusalem destroyed? "Because her people acted according to the law, and did not act beyond the requirements of the law."[14] Thus, as was mentioned in the quote from Nachmanides, the "right and the good" often entails going beyond the letter of the law. Judges are given discretion as to how to interpret the law. The Bible does advocate the institution of the death penalty for a number of violations, especially for murder. The *Talmud* then goes on to interpret as to when the death penalty can be prescribed. For instance, it is ruled that two witnesses are required to testify not only that they witnessed the act for which the criminal has been charged but that they had warned him beforehand that if he carried out the act he would be executed, and he had to accept the warning, stating his willingness to commit the act despite his awareness of its consequences. The criminal's own confession is not accepted as evidence. Moreover, circumstantial evidence is not admitted. In effect the death penalty is hardly ever instituted. "A Sanhedrin (the ancient high court in Israel) that puts a man to death once in seven years is called destructive. Rabbi Eliezer ben Azariah says: even once in seventy years. Rabbi Akiba and Rabbi Tarfon say: had we been in the Sanhedrin none would ever have been put to death. Rabban Simeon ben Gamaliel says: they would have multiplied shedders of blood in Israel, (implying that issuing the death penalty increases the 'shedding of blood')."[15]

An even more compelling example comes from the *midrashim* related to the law in Torah that stipulates that "execution by stoning" is the punishment to be given to the "rebellious son."[16] The Rabbis have a major issue with that law. In Talmud, Tractate *Sanhedrin* (71a), they basically reject the reading and offer a multitude of *midrashic* readings that in fact make the case un-prosecutable. The Rabbis stipulate that the boy must steal his parents' money, that he must consume huge quantities of meat and wine, that his parents must be similar in voice and appearance, etc. etc. "In fact, the *Talmud* ultimately declares that there never was nor ever could be a rebellious son."[17]

The story of Jeptha's daughter adds a chilling note to the plethora of stories regarding the necessity of going beyond the letter of the law. Jeptha, a battle commander whose personality is in disrepute, makes a vow that if he wins the battle with the Ammonites, he will sacrifice, i.e. make a burnt offering to God, the first living thing that comes out of his house. He had thought it would be a goat or a sheep, but instead it is his daughter. The law states that if a person makes a vow to God, then that person must follow through. There are circumstances by which the vow can be annulled.

> Jeptha's daughter seeks to find various ways by which to nullify the vow. She tells her father that the Torah commands man to bring offerings of cattle, from the herd or from the flock (Lev. 1:2) rather than human sacrifices. Her father replies that his vow was couched in general wording, "whatever comes out of the door of my house." His daughter's response to this argument is that the Patriarch Jacob also made a general vow: "and of all that You give me, I will set aside a tithe for You" (Gen. 28:22), and although twelve sons were later born to him, he did not sacrifice a single one of his offspring. But this argument also fails to convince Jephthah. The daughter is therefore presented—in contrast to her father—as conversant in the laws of the Torah and the stories of the Bible. She argues with her father like a sharp-witted Torah scholar who employs logical reasoning. Unfortunately, none of her arguments succeeds in deterring her father from fulfilling his vow.
>
> When the daughter realized that her father would not listen to her arguments, she asked him to go to the Sanhedrin since perhaps they would find a pretext for releasing him from his vow; but the Holy One, blessed be He, hid the law from them. The Rabbis are also critical of the members of that entire generation, on account of whose arrogance Jephthah's daughter died. In their opinion, the vow could have been annulled, for a *Tannaitic halakhah* states that something not fit to be offered on the altar shall not be so offered and accordingly possesses no sanctity (that it would have as a designated sacrifice) (*Lev. Rabbah* 37:4; *Midrash Aggadah*, ed. Buber, Lev. 27). Moreover, Phinehas the High Priest lived in that generation and he could have annulled the vow. Phinehas, however, said: "I am a High Priest, the son of a High Priest; shall I debase myself and go to Jephthah, who is a boor?" Jephthah likewise said: "I am the head of the tribes of Israel, shall I

debase myself by going to a commoner?" The midrash comments: "And between those two, the unfortunate girl was lost."[18]

Both Jeptha and Phineas, the high priest, are punished for their lapse in allowing the death to occur. Phineas loses his prophetic inspiration and Jeptha's body parts become scattered throughout the land.

It is interesting to note that in Rabbinic literature it was stipulated that judges should be parents as being a parent usually means that one is more predisposed to be compassionate. "The Talmud teaches that only fathers could become members of the Sanhedrin. Further, a very old man could not be on the Sanhedrin for, as Rashi˙ explains, he would have "forgotten the pain of raising children and so would not be compassionate. One who did not have children might turn out to be cruel. Fathers who knew firsthand the "pain of raising children" would be more likely to empathize with people."[19] The legal system is in place but there is wide latitude in interpretation. The emphasis is always placed on compassion, on restoration of communal and personal relationships.

Compassion and Mercy

The Hebrew word for compassion is *rahamim* which is derived from the word *rehem* meaning womb. (See above note regarding Hebrew roots; here the root is the three letter "r-khe-m), thus the word compassion at its very root is an homage to the feminine, an idea that compassion is rooted in and best expressed in the mother-child relationship. This compassion though rooted in the family bonds transcends them and encompasses all human relationships.[20] The *midrash* as to why the stork is not considered a kosher bird illuminates this very concept.˙ It is

---

˙ Rabbi Shlomo Yitzchaki, better known by acronym Rashi, 11th century Torah scholar.

suggested in the *midrash* that birds that are considered kosher have characteristics that are considered beneficial. So, for example, birds of prey are not considered kosher. The stork, however, is considered beneficial, and kind, it cares deeply for its young. Its name in Hebrew is *Hassidah* with the root being *hesed* implying that the bird is noted for its caring character. However, its character is considered limited.

Rashi considered the case of the *hasidah* and, based upon a *Talmudic* passage in *Chulin*, explains the limitation in the quality of the *hasidah* that, despite its connection to charity and kindness, keeps it from being kosher. Like a distant cousin in a good and decent family, the *chasidah* does share the chasid's kindness and piety. However, the *chasidah* is kind, but only *to her own kind*. She is charitable, but only to her own kind. She is caring, but only to her own kind.[21]

As stated above, care and compassion are indeed rooted in family bonds but in order for the individual to lead an ethical life he or she must go beyond the family and use these attributes to encompass all relationships. Thus, the stork does not meet these requirements and is therefore not considered a kosher bird.

In Judaism since we are made in God's image, we are commanded to imitate God's attributes, none more important than "compassion." "as He is merciful, so be you merciful." [22] God is often referred to as *HaRachaman* or the compassionate one.

As defined by the *Encyclopedia Judaica*: "MERCY (Heb. רַחֲמִים), a feeling of compassion tempered with love, which engenders forgiveness and forbearance in man and which stimulates him to deeds of charity and kindness." The following *midrash* shows even further that compassion is to be shown even to enemies as it is then possible to make peace, that is to restore connection between human beings."

---

* There are very defined laws as to what makes an animal or a fish kosher, not so with fowl.

Rabbi Alexandri said: Two ass drivers who hated each other were walking on a road when the ass of one lay down under its burden. His companion saw it, and at first he passed on.

But then he reflected: Is it not written in the Torah: "When you see the ass of your enemy lying under its burden....nevertheless, raise it with him?" (Exodus 23:5). So he returned, lent a hand, and helped his enemy in loading and unloading. He began talking to his enemy: "Release a bit here, pull up over there, unload over here." Thus peace came about between them, so that the driver of the overloaded ass said, "Did I not suppose that he hated me? But look how compassionate he was with me." By and by, the two entered an inn, ate and drank together, and became fast friends. What caused them to make peace and to become fast friends? Because one of them kept what is written in the Torah. Hence: "Thou hast established harmony."[23]

Jewish concepts of justice include the idea of strict justice as indicated in the words *din* and *mishpat*. However, God's attribute of mercy or compassion complements justice used in this sense. "This combination of justice and mercy in God is denoted in the two names of God, *Elohim*, and *YHWH*, the first of which designates justice, the second, mercy. God resolves the tension between strict judgment and mercy in favor of the latter."[24] Just as this quality of mercy in God is juxtaposed and often overrides justice, so it was in Jewish law administered by courts and judges as evidenced in sacred text. (See previous section on the word *Tsedek*.)

The quality of mercy is an essential attribute of God. We are called upon to emulate God and manifest this quality in our daily lives. The Rabbis go to great lengths to teach how mercy can be inculcated and augmented. For example, the laws prohibiting killing an animal and its young on the same day[25] are in place according to Nachmanides·, in order to further cultivate the quality of mercy. The pain of the mother if

---

· Rabbi Moses ben Nahman, better known as Nachmanides, (194-1270) noted Rabbinical scholar.

she views the slaying of her young is taken into consideration. Animals are not considered any different from human beings in care, love, and tenderness for their young. People must be restrained and prevented from killing the two together. "The reason for the prohibition is to eradicate cruelty and pitilessness from man's heart-real reason is to cultivate in us the quality of mercy that we may not become cruel for cruelty envelops the entire personality of man"[26]

The prophets railed against those nations that showed no compassion; for the lack of compassion marks out a people as "cruel" (Jer. 6:23). The Chaldeans were without compassion in that they slaughtered the young and helpless'); and Edom is castigated for having cast away all compassion." The Amalekites were to have their name blotted out from the annals of history, because they killed the stragglers, the weak, and the helpless who were not able to defend themselves.

Forgiveness

Perhaps the best way to understand the concept of mercy or compassion is to explore the nature of forgiveness in Jewish theology. Here too one finds the primacy of relationship. To fully comprehend the nature of forgiveness, which is contained in the nature of compassion (see quote on first page of the chapter) it is essential to elucidate three major tenets. One, we are commanded to follow in God's ways by imitating the divine attributes, such as compassion. "You shall be holy for I the Lord your God am holy."[27]

The second tenet is that the role of forgiveness is ultimately to restore and repair a relationship that has broken down because of the offense. The third is that there is no forgiveness without repentance on the part of the wrongdoer.""" "Our masters taught: all the aforementioned

---

' 2 Chronicles 36:17
" Amos 1:11
"" Here we find a major difference between Judaic and Christian concepts.

fines compensate only for the humiliation suffered by the victim. As for the hurt done to his feelings, even if the offender brings all the rams of Nebiaoth in the world, the offense is not forgiven until the offender asks for pardon."[28] What I have been highlighting all along here is how Judaic text elevates the vital importance of relationship, that notions of justice, *tsedek,* include relationship, that the ultimate restoration of relationship is the goal of justice, that harsher constructs of strict justice have to be weighed alongside the call to compassion, mercy. I would remind the reader here of Carol Gilligan's notion that the highest level of ethical virtue is that of care for the self-other relationship where care for the self is an absolute part of the equation. So, when others behave cruelly, without compassion, toward oneself or toward another Judaic text asserts that one should not show mercy toward that person or nation. The Talmud states the following: "whoever shows mercy for the merciless will end up becoming merciless toward men committed to mercy."[29] If we are committed to a just and merciful world, to offer compassion where cruelty has been committed does not repair a broken relationship, it in fact perpetuates the cruelty.

The noted African American author and academic, Julius Lester who had converted to Judaism, wrote a eulogy for Elie Wiesel. In the eulogy Lester quoted from a conversation he had had with Wiesel wherein Wiesel quoted the above-mentioned Talmudic passage. Lester went on to state how liberating this idea was for him, for he had suffered greatly at the hands of some white men, and it was right to hate them because it enabled him to freely love others, and in a Jewish context to be merciful, indeed it is incumbent upon the person to forgive when the transgressor is fully contrite.˙

˙ Nelson Mandela was able to achieve the almost unachievable, reconciliation in South Africa through his "truth and reconciliation" panels whereby former officials and perpetrators of white supremacy expressed remorse.

Endnotes: Chapter 4

[1] Friedell, op. cit.

[2] Deut. 6:18.

[3] Nahmanides (Rabbi Moshe ben Nahman (1194-1270) Talmudist and Kabbalist comment on the Biblical quote from Deuteronomy 6:18.

[4] Jason Ripley, "Covenantal Concepts of Justice and Righteousness" *Journal of Ecumenical Studies*, 2001, v. 38 no. 1, p. 95.

[5] Zech. 7:9-10.

[6] Jon D. Levinson, *Creation and the Persistence of Evil*, Princeton: Princeton University Press, 1988.

[7] *Midrash B'Midbar Rabbah,* cited by Rabbi Bradley Shavit Artson in "My Jewish Learning," commentary on *Parshat Nasso.*

[8] Ezek: 5, Job 1:10-1.

[9] Gen. 6:9.

[10] *Midrash Tanhuma* quoted by Zornberg, op. cit., p. 60

[11] Suzanne Last Stone, "Justice, Mercy, and Gender in Rabbinic Thought", *Cardozo Studies in Law and Literature*, vol.8, no.1, 1966.

[12] From *Genesis Rabah,* cited in Hayim Nachman Bialik and Yehoshua Rawinsky, op. cit.

[13] Ibid.

[14] *Talmud Baba Metzia*, quoted in Heschel, op. cit.

[15] *The Mishnah, Makkot, 1.4-2.2* Translated from the Hebrew by Herbert Danby, Peabody, Mass.: Hendrickson Publishers, 2011.

[16] *Parshat Ki Tetse*, Deut.chapters 22-25.

[17] Rabbi Sid Slivko, commentary on *parshat Ki Tetse.*

[18] https://jwa.org/encyclopedia/article/jephthas-daughter-midrash-and-aggadah

[19] Stone, op. cit.

[20] *Talmud* cited in *Encyclopedia Judaica.*

[21] https://www.ou.org/torah/parsha/parsha-from-ou/the-stork-and-what-its-name-means-for-us/.

[22] Mel Scult, (ed), *Communings of the Spirit, The Journals of Mordecai M. Kaplan, vol. 2*, Detroit: Wayne State University Press, 2016.

[23] *Midrash Tanhuma, Mishpatime*, #1.

[24] *Encyclopedia Judaica*

[25] Levit.22:28.

[26] Nachmanides https://choosemosaic.org/services/this-shabbat/shabbat-commentary-45/.

[27] Levit. 11:44-45, 19:2, 20:7.

[28] Bialik and Ravnitzky, op. cit., p. 645.

[29] Cited by Elie Wiesel in *A Jew Today*, New York: Random House, 1978. p.206.

Chapter 5

Autonomy Within
A Relational Context

"It is not good for man to be alone"[1]

"All Jews are responsible for one another"[2]

A sense of self that is constituted by relationships forms the very basis of a morality of care. It is thus often alleged that the very idea of moral autonomy cannot be conceived of within the context of care ethics. Care ethics conceives of the person as an "embedded self." Philosopher Jean Keller sees the person, the moral agent is "one who is always embedded in relations of flesh and blood and is partly constituted by these relations."[3] We may then ask, how can this person act autonomously? In my view, this question of autonomy depends on how the term is defined. Traditionally, in the West autonomy is defined in Kantian terms as being the property of an individual rational self-conceived as a self-contained unit. One can conjure up a vision of such an individual as "seemingly unfettered" standing alone looking to the stars. In point of fact, it is an ideal of Western culture that a self-actualized individual is one who is self-sufficient, independent and self-reliant. In her groundbreaking work *In a Different Voice*, Carol Gilligan links the concept of autonomy with the notion of a self that is separate, one traditionally linked to Western masculine development. As discussed in Chapter 2, Gilligan based her work on psychoanalyst Nancy

Chodorow's analysis of Western trajectories of development, In Chodorow's assessment, male development is based on defensive emphatic separation from the mother while girls grow up with a sense of self that can be articulated as "self-in-relation" where self-other boundaries are permeable. Autonomy, as Jean Keller states, includes "self-governance, the ability to exercise control over one's life through the choices one makes; a person must first develop the capacity to reflect critically on one's reasons for action, that is to question why one is acting in a particular manner and to assess whether it is really in accordance with one's actual beliefs, values or desires-can one take responsibility for this or that action while retaining one's self-respect."[4] This sense of an autonomous self, an "I" from a relational perspective must originally develop from a "we," specifically from the relationships between parent and child. This is what object-relations theorist, Margaret Mahler delineates as the stage of separation-individuation, a stage that slowly develops from the maternal matrix that characterizes the symbiotic stage.* Furthermore this "I" once developed, can expand, when ego boundaries are not defensively erected, to encompass the "we." Although not quite explicit that Hillel's notion of "I" is relationally determined, the idea that we are selves-in-relation is beautifully expressed by him. "If I am not for myself, who will be for me? But if I am only for myself, what am I?"[5] This famous aphorism quintessentially illuminates the concept of moral autonomy within a relational self.** As such this aphorism is entirely commensurate with Gilligan's notion of "self-in-relation." Self is part of the relation! Neither Hillel nor Gilligan are talking about self-abnegation, the giving up of one's self for the good of another regardless of the impact or consequences to one's self.

---

* I have already delineated some of the theoretical as well as the neurological material in previous sections, specifically Chapter 2.

** I am making the assumption based on my readings that Hillel's "self" is at least partially constituted by relationship.

The Hebrew word for "I" is usually *ani*. The word *anokhi* is an alternative word for "I" that is sometimes used in Jewish sacred text instead of *ani*. Why is *anokhi* used in place of ani? Various Rabbinic commentaries explicate the significance of *anokhi*, namely its inherent invocation of the self-in-relation. "*Anokhi* is the proclamation of intimate nearness between the speaker and the listener. It is an "I" that encompasses "others," and is thereby infinitely more whole. If we want to emulate God, we cannot stay within the isolated ego. We must start with the self (*ani*), but then move out into the world of others. By so doing, we free them and ourselves from bondage and reveal a greater self (*anokhi*). It is a self that is simultaneously a part of a greater whole."[6] The use of the word *anokhi* as self-in-relation becomes further clarified if we look to words used in Deuteronomy to assess personal and collective responsibility. The Torah *parshah* of *Re'eh* in Deuteronomy begins with the words: *Reeh anokhi noten lifneichem hayom bracha u-klalah.* "See: this day I set before you blessing and curse."[7] This passage suggests that the fate of any family, community, or nation—or the fate of the entire world—is the aggregate of each person's individual decisions to steer the world ever so slightly in the direction of curse or in the direction of blessing. The Rabbis note that the word *Re'eh* – 'See' – is a singular verb, while the word *lifneichem* 'before you' – is in plural (i.e., meaning 'before all of you.') We are individuals but also we are part of a collective; our fate is determined in part by the decisions of others, but each of us has more power than we realize to steer the world towards blessing.

Autonomy: Individual and Relational

The Oven of Akhnai

The Talmudic story of "The oven of akhnai,"[8] which is set around the early 2nd century CE), offers an interesting juxtaposition of God's lauding of human autonomy with God's castigation of dehumanization and indifference. The story concerns a dispute over whether a particular oven is "clean" or "unclean" and includes participants in the argument retaliating against the Rabbi who opposed them in a way that severely diminishes his humanity and denotes a total lack of empathy and respect. In the story Rabbi Eliezer asserts that the oven is "clean" and all the other sages assert that it is unclean. Rabbi Eliezer asks "the heavens" to back him up and they do in the form of several miraculous events, such as a river running backwards and walls collapsing, However, the majority of the sages assert that the decision is "not in heaven" but rather that the Torah was given at Sinai and thus the decision is to be made here on earth by the majority of the sages. The *midrash*[9] goes on to say upon hearing the dispute and the decision God laughed with joy saying "my children have defeated me." The effect here is that God applauds human autonomy and encourages it. However, the fact is that these sages then destroy all the previous responses and verdicts of Rabbi Eliezer. In fact, they burn his work (as per Tova Hartman's discussion of the relevant *Talmudic* text) strip him of his position, and cast him out from among his people. What then ensues are a number of disasters, including withering crops and even the death of one of the sages, Rabbi Gamliel. Hartman[10] infers that this destruction is in fact a response to the severing of the relationship between Rabbi Eliezer and his people and the sages and God.˙ It can be averred that autonomy must be within the context of relationship and that destruction and violence follows from the cutting of these emotional relational ties.

Ma Tovu

Ma Tovu is a prayer said upon entering synagogues that is taken from the Bible, specifically from Numbers 24:5. The English translation can

---

˙ The severity of the response denotes an emotional decision rather than a rational one.

be rendered as "How Goodly are your tents O Jacob, your dwelling places O Israel." The story in Numbers is that the prophet Balaam is hired by King Balak of Moab to curse the Israelites as they were journeying through his land on their way to Canaan. They had already defeated other kings and Balak was afraid. Balaam goes to curse the Israelites as they were camped in their tents but is so taken with how they related to one another that instead of cursing, Balaam blessed them using the above-mentioned words. The *midrash*[11] specifically hones in on the fact that Balaam saw that the flaps of the tents were placed such that each family was given privacy, no one could look into the tent of another. Boundaries were meticulously observed, respect for individual families was prized.

Tower of Babel

At the beginning of the story depicted in the Biblical episode of The Tower of Babel,[12] we are told that the earth speaks a single language. The people have agreed to build a city with a tower that will ascend to heaven. The implication of the tower is that the people see themselves as all-powerful, omnipotent and are in effect challenging God. God understands and is immediately aware of their motivation and imposes a punishment, "confounding the language" and dispersing the people over the face of the earth.

If we look once more to the object-relations theory of Margaret Mahler, we see that she has posited a developmental sequence where the infant must first go through a symbiotic stage with the mother, a stage of psychic merging with the mother, where the child feels itself together with the mother as all-powerful. The mother intuitively understands the child's rudimentary language and interprets h/her needs. French psychoanalyst Julia Kristeva˙ describes this speech as

---

˙ Julia Kristeva, Bulgarian/French psychoanalyst (b. 1941).

55

semiotic discourse, a language of symbiosis and connection specifically as fusion with the mother. The next stage in Mahler's theory is that of separation-individuation where the infant slowly emerges from symbiosis and becomes a separate individual. Here language slowly becomes coherent and rational.

According to the *midrash,*[13] God did not punish the Tower generation as he did with the flood generation because the people showed a love for one another. If we continue to look through the lens of psychoanalysis, we could state that their love for one another was at an early developmental level, they were in fact fused with each other. They spoke one language, the language of symbiotic connection, not of true relationship. God's imposition of many languages can be viewed as the imposition of ego boundaries. The "many languages" are the languages of separate, autonomous individuals. Now discourse between human beings, true relationships can take place at a more advanced level.

Geneivat Da'at

Thou shall not steal is the 8th commandment of the Decalogue. Many types of theft are delineated in that particular commandment, such as kidnapping, theft of property, and wages. However, some of the Rabbis of the *Talmud* state that the most egregious type of theft can be articulated as *geneivat da'at,* or theft of the mind. "The sages believed that there are seven types of thieves and, of these, the most egregious is the one who "steals the minds" of people."[14] While it is difficult to specifically define, theft of the mind implies the transgression of personal boundaries, i.e. one individual usurping the autonomy of the other. Examples given in the *midrash* include the following: one should not invite a friend for dinner if he knows that the friend cannot come, one should not offer gifts to someone whom s/he knows will not accept them, one should not open a bottle of wine for someone making them believe that it was done for their honor when, in reality, the bottle was sold to a shopkeeper and was going to be opened anyway. The underlying reason for the transgression in all of these cases is deceit. In each example, the transgressor is deceiving the person and in so doing is subverting their ability to act autonomously. The thief, in effect, has stolen the mind of the other. The relationship is compromised; it becomes transactional rather than truly interpersonal.

According to philosopher Michael Slote,[15] autonomy has two components: respect for the "autonomous other" and an empathetic understanding of his/her needs. Empathy is a product of the "embedded self." True autonomy is then not based on a defensive narcissistic self-sufficiency, i.e. not on an autonomy that is built defensively as a reaction against the symbioses of mother-child fusion but on true object-relations. In the example of the Oven of Akhnai autonomy is lauded but when it's at the expense of relationships destruction follows. *Ma Tovu* signifies the opposite. Here Balaam is about the curse the encampment of the Israelites but when he sees the nature of the relationships that exist among the people and their respect for each other's boundaries, blessings follow. The Tower of Babel illustrates how an ethic of care can only emerge when people have advanced in their development such that true relatedness can exist. The idea that is elucidated in *Gevinaat Ha Da'at* is that individual boundaries cannot be transgressed, people are never to be seen nor treated as "means" to an end. Jewish ethics compels the individual to see an "other" as an individual made in the image of God and thus must relate to them in empathic understanding as autonomous individuals. In his commentary on *Parshat Naso*,[16] Rabbi Jonathan Sacks discusses why the Torah uses the word *naso* here translated as "count" as in to count the census. The usually translation for that word has to do with "lifting the head." What Rabbi Sacks says is that by the use of the word "*naso*" the Torah is enjoining us not to see people as numbers. "At the very moment when one might be maximally tempted to see people as "just numbers" –

namely, when taking a census, as here – the Israelites were commanded to "lift people's heads," to raise their spirits, to make them feel they counted as individuals, not numbers in a mass, ciphers in a crowd." Sacks in this same commentary goes on to reiterate that we are also interdependent, no "I" without the "we."

Endnotes: Chapter 5

[1] Gen. 2:18.

[2] Babylonian Talmud: Shavuot 39a.

[3] Jean Keller, "Autonomy, Relationality, and Feminist Ethics," *Hypatia* vol. 12, no. 2, 1997, pp.152-164.

[4] Ibid.

[5] Ethics of the Fathers, 1:14.

[6] Rabbi Yakov Astor, "Me, Myself and I," *Ethics of the Fathers.* 1:14 found at http://www.aish.com/sp/pg/48893292.html).

[7] Deut. 11:26.

[8] Talmud, Tractate *Bava Metzia* 59a-b.

[9] Cited by Tova Hartman, op. cit.

[10] Ibid.

[11] Cited by Ravnitsky and Bialik, op. cit.

[12] Gen. 11.

[13] Cited by Ravnitsky and Bialik, op. cit.

[14] *Tosefta Bava Kama* 7:3.

[15] Michael Slote, *Ethics of Care and Empathy,* New York and London: Routledge, 2007.

[16] Rabbi Jonathan Sacks, http://rabbisacks.org/lifting-heads-naso-5778/ .

Chapter 6

Ezer K'negedo, Moses, *Hevrutah* Study

In chapter 5, I discussed the notion found both in feminist moral thinking and in Jewish sacred text of an embedded, i.e. internally interconnected, yet autonomous self that feels responsive to both the needs of the self and of others.

The trajectory of infant development that leads to this conception of "self" is one in which there are significant others (most often the mother but not exclusively so) that allows for the early psychological fusion (symbiosis, in Mahler's words) of baby with mother. Starting at about 18 months, through a series of difficult steps, the baby psychologically separates from the mother. The successful mother provides the child with the type of environment that allows for this pattern of separation, rapprochement (regressive return) and then additional separation in order to successfully develop culminating in the emergence of a self that remains internally connected yet autonomous. This "good enough" parenting˙ thus results in an autonomous individual with permeable boundaries. These fluid boundaries between self and other enable the child and then the adult with an ability to empathize with another human being. This empathic ability is the very basis of a morality of care.

˙ Term coined by D.W. Winnicott. See Chapter 2.

In chapters 3 and 4 the Hebrew words for justice, compassion, and care along with Biblical and *midrashic* examples were elucidated to show how morality is construed to augment, enhance and restore connection to significant others, to fellow Jews and then expands to all humankind in general. In this chapter I present the idea that it is empathy and the emotional, behavioral, and cognitive components thereof that underlies the precepts discussed. This chapter also argues that this capacity can be inculcated and augmented through the reading and communal discussion and interpretation of the text. That is radical listening to the other in any situation, but especially in context of textual discussion is the way of fulfilling and enhancing our covenantal relationship with God. To again cite a quote taken from Laurie Zoloth from the beginning of Chapter 1:

> This method (listening, reading, and interpreting text in a community) dictates that human life is essential, that human flourishing is rooted not simply in justice, but in love and mutuality and that righteousness (*tsedek*) and lovingkindness *(hesed)* are at the heart of human survival.

If we now look to Jewish texts and how the notion of "self" is depicted therein, we find, although not explicitly stated, the notion of "self" as "self-in-relation" is implicit and comes across via a multitude of sources. Issues related to impositions of boundary and notions of care are in the text literally from the beginning. It all begins from the primordial, the *tohu v'vohu* translated into English as the "unformed void," of the Biblical text. Light separates from dark, the waters from the earth (upper waters from the lower waters). Modern Biblical scholar, Avivah Gottlieb Zornberg[1] discusses a *midrash* on the idea of separation. Separation is generally achieved at some sacrifice. When, for instance, the lower waters are separated from the higher waters on the second day of creation, the lower waters are described in *midrashic* sources as "weeping." The formation of plants and animals follow. The physical world emanates, i.e. emerges, from the original *tohu v'vohu*, cosmos from chaos.

The concept of separation with regard to the human being and sense of self is further delineated in *Bereshit*, Genesis (1:27). If we go back to the Biblical text, "And God created man in His image, in the image of God He created him; male and female He created them." Some *midrashic* interpretations had this original being as both male and female, as androgynous.[2] Rashi stipulates that "God created him (the first human being) first with two faces, and separated them."[3] Ramban* further comments it was important to realize man as two matched creatures, rather than as one androgynous being because, "God saw that it was good that his helpmate should stand in front of him." For Ramban, man as alone and autonomous is "not good" because he would live a static, unchanging and unwilled life. There is in this quote a reverberation from the original *tohu v'vohu*, where there is only unity, no separation, there is no change, no growth, no life! Implied in the text is the notion of original connection (male and female He created them) and then separation into man and woman. Yet in separating while the original physical connection is lost what we find is that the psychological connection, the sense of self as self-in-relation is gained. Furthermore the Bible says that God created Eve as *ezer k'negdo*," a helper who stands against him but also in front of him. This strangely worded "stance" allows for mirroring, reflection, imitation, and confrontation as well as can simultaneously help to *augment the* underlying concept of true empathy and care that implies respect for

---

* Another name used for Nachmanides
" Kenegdo, translated as "fitting" has confrontational implications, so that he may see her and separate from her, and unite with her, according to his will (Ramban 2:18).

"the other" in his or her individuality. The ultimate result being the formation of new life!

Moses

Using the Biblical figure of Moses as a means of further elucidating this text we can see how "self-in-relation" is depicted and revealed in his person, his enormous capacity to feel empathy, to then act and ultimately in his leadership capacity. I use Moses here as he is, in fact, the figure, the leader, the one who enabled the transformation of the Israelites into a nation, a nation that partners with God to live lives that embody the ideals and laws initially set down in Torah, i.e. to be a holy people. It takes a leader such as Moses to unify his people under the same faith that organizes their life in relation to God but also in relation to each other. Abraham, Isaac and Jacob are the fathers of the religion because they spoke directly with God on the original tenets of faith. But they each made the covenant with God on an individual basis. Adam and Eve are the father and mother of all humanity, the three founding fathers and mothers are the founding parents of the covenant. Moses is, however, the founder of the nation.

There is the Biblical text and the many legends surrounding the birth and rearing of Moses. All attest to the fact that Jocheved, Moses' biological mother reared him until about three months of age by hiding him from those carrying out Pharoah's decree that all male Israelite babies should be killed at birth. After the three months, she put the infant in a basket to float on the Nile and gave Miriam, Moses' sister the order to watch over the baby. Pharoah's daughter, known in later texts as Batya, (daughter of God) comes to the river, sees the infant and is smitten by him. The *Talmud* states that when she opened the "box," and saw the child, she immediately sensed God's presence. She retrieves the basket, tells her women that she will adopt the child and rear him as her own. Miriam, who had been watching over the child, speaks to

Pharaoh's daughter and volunteers to find the baby a wet nurse. Jocheved, Moses' biological mother, is hired to fulfill this role. According to *midrash*,[4] Jocheved stayed to nurse Moses until he was two or three years old. There are a myriad of legends that attest to the worth of Jocheved, both as an individual and as a mother. She is sometimes identified with one of the midwives who delivered babies in defiance of Pharoah's edict risking death in the process. All of Jocheved's children were exemplary, each in his or her own capacity was deemed a prophet. Based on the actions of Aaron, Miriam, and Moses, we can infer that Jocheved was an exceptional mother who embodied and transmitted empathic care and concern to her children via her loving attentiveness and attunement to their wants and needs. In addition, Jocheved, whose name (Hebrew *yokheved)* apparently means *YHWH* ˙ is glory," is notable as the first person in the Bible to have a name with the divine element *yah,* a shortened form of *YHWH.* The tradition that Moses announces to the Israelites that *YHWH* is the name of their God[5] is thus embedded in his maternal lineage: if his mother bears *YHWH's* name, Moses learned it from her.[6] But moreover, *YHWH* is forever associated with Jocheved. The sustainer and nurturer of life is linked with God, with mother. The meaning of God is life. Moses had an internalized model (working model) of a caring mother that represented the importance of caring for people and that people deserve that care, compassion, and sustenance.

To illuminate Moses' capacity to empathize, to assert a specific type of leadership, what is known in the psychology literature as transformative leadership, we can look to the concept of attachment theory. I discussed attachment theory in Chapter 2. Again, according to attachment theory, which grew from the works of John Bowlby and Mary Ainsworth, "attachment in infants is primarily a process of *proximity seeking* to an identified *attachment figure* in situations of

---

˙ *YHWH* is used to denote God's name that is prohibited from being pronounced.

perceived distress or alarm for the purpose of survival. Infants become attached to adults who are sensitive and responsive in social interactions with the infant, and who remain as consistent caregivers for some months during the period from six months to two years of age. Parental responses lead to the development of patterns of attachment which in turn lead to 'internal working models' which will guide the individual's feelings, thoughts, and expectations in later relationships."[7] Much research has been successful in linking secure attachment to a number of important social developmental factors. Specifically there is research directly referring to secure attachment as the basis for empathy from early childhood to adulthood.

There is also brain research to back this claim.[8] Thus, from the fact that Moses' true mother was brought to feed the baby, not just any wet nurse, and that she most likely reared Moses until he was at least two, we can infer that attachment, i.e. secure attachment, was indeed inculcated in the infant Moses. From current research in cognitive psychology and neuropsychology linking attachment with empathy we give credence to the fact that many of Moses' behaviors, especially towards the Hebrew slaves, are motivated by empathy. Moses grows up in the palace as he is the adopted son of Pharaoh's daughter. The Bible says: "Sometime ... when Moses had grown up, he went out to his kinsfolk and witnessed their labors."[9] The *midrash*[10] asks "How did he feel as "he looked on"? As he looked on their burdens he wept, saying "Woe is me for your servitude! Would that I could die for you!' Avivah Zornberg cites Rashi[11] "He gave his eyes and his heart to be distressed over them." The Biblical text uses the word "kinfolk" and "brothers" to describe the slaves. Even though he was brought up in the palace he identifies with the Hebrews in Goshen. Zornberg goes on "Moses' seeing is Moses allowing himself to be affected, to suffer with those who are unexpectedly called 'his brothers.' Moses' first significant act of maturity is an act of empathy with those who seem, physically, socially, and existentially, so different from him." Zornberg continues "It is on the basis of that vulnerable empathy that he then 'sees' the Egyptian taskmaster battering one of his brother." Moses reacts and kills the taskmaster. This empathy that was first inculcated through his attachment to his mother, impels Moses to act, to kill the taskmaster. "This memory of our own best moments of caring and being cared for sweeps over us as a feeling-as an "I must" - in response to the plight of the other: I recognize the feeling and remember what has followed it in my own best moments. I have a picture of those moments in which I was cared for and in which I cared, and I may reach toward this memory and guide my conduct by it if I wish to do so."[12] This first adult act performed because of empathy ultimately leads Moses to the role that God ordained for him.

Empathy

From modern work in psychology and neuroscience we can state that it is empathy and the emotional, cognitive and behavioral components thereof, that provides the basis for the multitude of voices of care, pity, compassion and justice, i.e. *tsedek, din, mishpat,* and *hesed,* and *rahamim* that we find in Jewish sacred text. Developmental psychologist Martin Hoffman defines empathy as "an affective response that is more appropriate for another's situation than one's own." Hoffman continues: "empathy is the spark of human concern for others, the glue that makes social life possible."[13] The synthesis between affect and cognition forms the foundations for what philosopher Michael Slote[14] calls the virtue of empathetic caring. Affect is present almost from birth as elaborated in the work on mirror neurons. Cognition, as it develops in the individual, enables a person to empathize with others who may not be immediately present. Together, empathy can embed within a moral principle. A society that reflects empathic caring in its institutions and laws as well as in its social customs and practices is what we call a just society or to state it in Biblical language a holy people. Again, we can see the very embodiment of this ideal in the character and behavior of Moses. I already have mentioned how he intervened in the struggle between the Egyptian taskmaster and the Hebrew slave. However, there are two other instances where Moses intervenes: 1) between two Jews who are engaged in a struggle and 2) between the daughters of Midianite priest, Jethro, and their accosters at the well. In the struggle between slave and overseer, he might have intervened because of the fact that he saw the Hebrew slave as "his brother." From the other two examples, however, we can infer that he fought on the side of the "just cause" on behalf of the oppressed. Thus, his empathic caring response was embedded in the moral principles of "justice" and "care."

In Chapter Four, I discussed the word *tsedek,* usually translated as "justice," as being totally commensurate with feminist ethics. Here I can now add to this assertion by stating that Jewish sacred text in the use of the word *tsedek* beautifully exemplifies Slote's idea of justice reflecting empathic caring motivation. One can also affirm that *tsedek* is also synonymous with "distributive justice" in that many of the tenets having to do with what is just have to do with caring for the poor, the widow, the orphan, the infirm. In the aforementioned chapter, I also showed that even in situations where words for strict justice are used (*mishpat, din*) they are always used in conjunction with mercy and compassion. Going beyond the letter of the law, *lifnei meshurat ha din*, can be viewed in terms of empathic caring in that there are instances where specific situations have impact and can even negate where strict law should be applied.

As per Martin Hoffman,[15] the virtue of empathetic caring needs to be inculcated through a specific type of moral education that he labels "induction" by parents, teachers and significant others in a child's life. Induction involves using empathy by using prompts such as "imagine how that child feels" in order to call attention to the hurt felt by others, or what Hoffman calls perspective taking. When disciplining the child, it should be incumbent on the parents to highlight others' perspectives, to point out another's distress, especially if it is caused by the child him/herself and to provide prosocial models. It is my contention that the critical interpretive study of Jewish sacred text specifically by methods of *hevruta* study is an exemplary way of illustrating Hoffman's idea of "induction." This method implies a close reading and active engagement by the interpreter rather than just a passive receiving of text. The reader must engage with the text as in a conversation by carefully "listening" as to what the text has to say. The result of this process becomes an experience "in which one encounters a text as an "other" involving her/his as well as the text's horizon in a dialectical process."[16] The education scholar Elie Holzer, articulates the case that the traditional method of *hevruta* study, where sacred text is read and discussed with a partner, enhances and augments not only the text itself but also the nature of the relationship with an "other" and thus has the potential to elevate the moral dimensions of both the text and the relationship.[17] I believe that this *hevruta* method mirrors the relationship that is set forth in Genesis between Adam and Eve as partners as *ezer k'negedo,* a helper who stands against him but in front as well. This type of relational learning involves a dialectical give and take with both the text and the partner that helps to give meaning and definition to the text, to each other and serves to elevate the moral relevance of the "voice of Sarah" that inheres in the text.

Endnotes: Chapter 6

[1] Zornberg, op. cit.
[2] Cited in Ravnitsky and Bialik, op. cit.
[3] Rashi on Bereshit.
[4] Cited in Ravnitsky and Bialik, op. cit.
[5] Ex. 6 1-8.
[6] Carol Meyers, *Women in Scripture*, New York: Houghten Mifflin, 2000.
[7] Bowlby, J. op. cit.
[8] Please refer to Chapter 2 in this text, specifically to the work of Allen Schore and Daniel Siegel.
[9] Ex. 2:11.
[10] Cited by Bialik and Ravnitsky, op. cit. p. 61.
[11] See Zornberg, op.cit,
[12] Nel Noddings, *Caring, a Feminine Approach to Ethics and Moral Education*, Berkeley and Los Angeles: University of California Press, 1984, p1.
[13] Martin Hoffman, *Empathy and Moral Development: Implications for Caring and Justice*, New York and Cambridge: Cambridge University Press, 2000.
[14] Slote, op. cit.
[15] Hoffman, *op* cit.
[16] Elie Holzer, "What Connects Good Teaching, Text Study and Hevruta Learning? A Conceptual Argument", *Journal of Jewish Education,* vol. 72, no.3, 2006.
[17] Ibid.

Chapter 7

Conclusion

In this work, I have attempted to dispel the notion that Judaism constitutes a religion of strict justice enshrined in immutable laws. On the contrary, close examination of Jewish sacred texts, including the Bible, *Talmud*, *Midrash* and others reveals the elevation of the virtues of care, empathy, and compassion all used in service to the inculcation, cementing and restoration of human relationships. Justice, particularly in its iteration as *tsedek*, embodies the primacy of relationship. It is human relationships, manifested interpersonally as well as on community and societal levels that is held as the highest moral achievement of humankind.

In 1982, in what would emerge as a modern paradigm shift, Carol Gilligan first alerted the fields of developmental psychology and of Western moral philosophy that their elevation of abstract moral principles as the highest stage of moral development was flawed. Her initial work, on which *In a Different Voice* was based, involved listening to girls' and women's voices when assessing and attempting to solve moral dilemmas. Through listening carefully, Gilligan came to hear "a different voice," that is a voice that attempted to solve these dilemmas based not on overarching abstract moral principles but one that looked to specific context, and that used qualities based on care and response to people in need as solutions. Her female subjects did not see the moral issues as "black" and "white" i.e. abstract ideas of right and wrong but instead as complex human dilemmas requiring solutions that caused the least amount of hurt. Gilligan, in her discussions, has used the example of a woman* who is facing the question as to whether or not to have an abortion. She is married with a small child. She has scoliosis of the spine and her husband is currently unemployed. Her doctor has told her that if she goes through with the pregnancy her spine will get worse and she'll be unable to work as a nurse. She is also Catholic. What is she to do? The dilemma is not construed as to whether or not abortion is morally wrong but rather how the woman can find the best solution given the specific circumstances of her situation.

When assessing the historical roots of Gilligan's assertions, philosophers see antecedents in the work of 18th century Scottish Enlightenment specifically in the work of David Hume and Francis Hutcheson on "sympathy." However, it has been my contention that this seemingly modern theory has its foundational source in Jewish sacred text. I have given multiple examples taken from Bible as well as *midrashic*, medieval, and contemporary sources that confirm that the ethical stance that has become known as "feminist ethics," or what I have called the "voice of Sarah," is in point of fact at the very heart of Jewish moral values.

Gilligan based her assertions regarding the development of the self on the works of object-relations theorists. These assertions were further validated by cognitive neuroscientists *vis a vis* their work in unraveling the essential part that primary caregivers play in advancing brain development. Through their work we have come to know that human beings are first and foremost relational beings. We know ourselves in early infancy first in relation to our significant others, our primary caregivers, and then we slowly emerge as autonomous beings still internally interconnected. It is this internal connection that allows for the permeability of self-other boundaries, which then allows for the formation of empathy. Jewish sacred text gives us multiple examples of how empathy is so foundational to Rabbinic thinking that it even plays

---

* A subject in one of Gilligan's abortion studies described by Gilligan in a YouTube video. https://www.youtube.com/watch?v=2W_9MozRoKE.

a part in our response to our enemies. During Passover, we deplete our full glass of wine by ten drops during the recitation of the ten plagues in order to diminish our joy as the Egyptians, also God's children, are destroyed. There is also a very telling *midrashic* story regarding the mother of Sisera, a commander of the Canaanite army bent on destroying the Israelites. Sisera is killed by the Biblical heroine, Jael. The *midrash* imagines Sisera's mother waiting for her son's return and then weeps upon hearing the news of his death. In point of fact according to some *midrashic* sources, the plaintive notes of the shofar that we hear on Rosh HaShannah mimic the very weeping of Sisera's mother.[1] So even on important holidays such as Passover and Rosh HaShannah we "hear" the voices of our enemies and they also form part of our collective memories.

Millennia before our modern knowledge of brain development, before the articulation of an "ethic of care," Rabbinic thinking stemming from the second century of the Common Era had a vision of society that was founded on concepts of relational justice. Justice was not based on punishment and retribution but was conceived of as restorative and whose augmentation was determined by care and response to the individual and to the community. Systems of laws were used to concretize and implement these values. However, sometimes the laws did not address and/ or meet the needs of the particular situation. Thus, the concept of *lifnei meshurat hadin* going beyond the letter of the law is seen as an essential component of restorative justice. This concept was discussed in an example in a previous chapter, where the relationship between husband and wife takes precedence over the law regarding the erasing the name of God. Another *midrashic* text suggests that Jerusalem's fall to the Romans in the first century of the Common Era was the result of judges who adhered too much to the letter of the law. This caused strife between people, severing relationships that formed the backbone of the society and inevitably leading to Jerusalem's demise.[2]

The gendered nature of this relational justice or ethic of care may best be highlighted in the book of Ruth.* All of the characters are noteworthy for their manifestation of *hesed,* of care in relation to one another. However, the book is named for Ruth who first shows her care in relation to her mother-in-law Naomi. Ruth goes way beyond what is expected of her by staying with Naomi despite Naomi's allowing her to leave. The Hebrew word used by Ruth when articulating her desire to stay text is translated as "cleave," the same word used in Genesis 2: 23, to describe how a husband and wife should "cleave" to one another. In other words, the "other" is still "bone of my bone and flesh of my flesh", or we are selves-in-relation, and one person cannot in good conscience leave another. It can be argued from a close reading of the text that Ruth actually serves as the example that elicits the other characters in the story to acts of *hesed.* It is the female who acts as a catalyst for relational justice just as it was the female who helped Gilligan illuminate the voice of care.

But even as Gilligan first "found" the moral voice of care in listening to girls and women when she did research, it is necessary to reiterate that the moral voice of care does not belong exclusively to women. Her book is not called in a woman's voice; the chosen title highlights instead a voice that differs from what had been previously considered the pinnacle of advanced moral thinking. It was, however, in listening to girls and women who had never been considered in the developmental literature, that Gilligan found this "other" profoundly human voice. Now, "care ethics" has become part of mainstream moral philosophy.

But the voice Gilligan heard alerts us to, is in fact much older although it too has been largely excised out of dominant interpretations. God tells Abraham in Genesis 21:12 to always listen to Sarah's voice. This voice, the voice of relationship forms the very basis of Jewish sacred text.

---

* See Chapter 3 in this text.

Endnotes: Chapter 7

[1] Ravnitsky and Bialik, op. cit.

[2] ibid.

BIBLIOGRAPHY

Ainsworth, Mary, "The Development of Infant-Mother Attachment" in *Review of Child Development Research*, Bettye Cardwell and Henry Ricciuti, (eds.), Chicago: University of Chicago Press. 1973.

Bialik, Hayim Nahman and Yehoshua Hana Ravnizky (eds.) *The Book of Legends (Sefer Ha-Agadah): Legends from the Talmud and Midrash*, William G. Braude (trans.) Riverhead. 1995.

Bowlby, John, *Attachment: Attachment Loss,* vol.1, New York: Basic Books, 1969.

_____, *Parent-Child Attachment and Healthy Human Development,* London: Routledge, 1988.

Campbell, Joseph, "The Power of Myth," 1988 TV series with correspondent Bill Moyers, PBS, 1988.

Chodorow, Nancy, *Feminism and Psychoanalytic Theory*, New Haven: Yale University Press, 1991.

_____, *The Reproduction of Mothering: Psychoanalysis and the Sociology of Gender,* Berkeley, University of California Press, 1999.

Clark, Gordon R. "The Word Hesed in the Hebrew Bible", *Journal for the Study of the Old Testament*, Thousand Oaks, California: Sage Publications, 1993.

Damasio, Antonio, *Descartes' Error: Emotion, Reason, and the Human Brain*, New York: Putnam, 1994.

_____, *The Feeling of What Happens: Body and Emotion in the Making of Consciousness*, New York: Harcourt, Brace, 1999.

Dawkins, Richard, *The God Delusion*, London: Transworld Publishers, 2007.

Friedell, Steven, "The Different Voice in Jewish Law," *Indiana Law Journal* vol. 67. Bloomington, 1992.

Frymer-Kensky, Tikva, *Reading the Women of the Bible.* New York: Schocken Press, 2002.

Gilligan, Carol, *In a Different Voice: Psychological Theory and Women's Development*, Cambridge: Harvard University Press, 1982.

Gilligan, Carol, Janie Victoria Ward, Jill McLean Taylor (eds.) *Mapping the Moral Domain,* Cambridge: Harvard University Press. 1988.

Ginzberg, Louis, *The Legends of the Jews* (7 volumes) Philadelphia: Jewish Publication Society, 1947.

Handelman, Susan, *Slayers of Moses,* Albany: SUNY press, 1983.

Hartman, Tova, and Charlie Buckholtz, *Are You Not a Man of God? Devotion, Betrayal, and Social Criticism in Jewish Tradition*, Oxford: Oxford University Press, 2014.

Hebrew-English Tanakh, Philadelphia: Jewish Publication Society, 2005.

Heschel, Abraham Joshua, *God in Search of Man, A Philosophy of Judaism,* New York: Farrar, Straus, Giroux, 1955.

Holtz, Barry, *Back to the Sources, Reading the Classic Jewish Texts,* New York: Summit Books, 1984.

Hoffman, Martin, *Empathy and Moral Development: Implications for Caring and Justice*, New York: Cambridge University Press, 2000.

Holzer, Elie, "What Connects Good Teaching, Text Study and Hevruta Learning? A Conceptual Argument," *Journal of Jewish Education* vol. 72, no.3 2006.

Iacoboni, Marco, *Mirroring People: The New Science of How We Connect with Others*, New York: Farrar, Strauss, and Giroux, 2008.

Keller, Jean, "Autonomy, Relationality, and Feminist Ethics," *Hypatia* vol. 12, no. 2, 1997.

Kohlberg, Lawrence, *The Philosophy of Moral Development: Moral Stages and the Idea of Justice*, San Francisco: Harper and Row, 1981.

Levinson, Jon, *Creation and the Persistence of Evil*, Princeton: Princeton University Press, 1988.

Meyers, Carol, *Women in Scripture*, New York: Houghten Mifflin, 2000.

Noddings, Nel, *Caring, a Feminine Approach to Ethics and Moral Education*, Berkeley: University of California Press, 1984.

Ramon, Einat, "The Matriarchs and the Torah of Hesed," *Nashim* 10. Fall 2005, pp.154-177.

Ripley, Jason, "Covenantal Concepts of Justice and Righteousness," *Journal of Ecumenical Studies,"* vol. 38, no.1, 2001.

Rubens, Richard, "Fairbairn's Structural Theory," http://www.columbia.edu/%7Err322/FAIRBAIRN.html.

Schept, Susan, "Feminist Ethics in Jewish Sacred Text," *Conservative Judaism,* vol. 57, no. 1, Fall 2004. pp. 21-29.

Schore, Allan N., "Effects of Secure Attachment Relationship on Right Brain Development Affect Regulation and Infant Mental Health," *Infant Mental Health Journal*, vol. 22, nos. 1-2, 2003, pp.7-66.

Scult, Mel, (ed), *Communings of the Spirit, The Journals of Mordecai M. Kaplan, Vol. 2*, Detroit: Wayne State University Press, 2016.

Shakespeare, William*, The Merchant of Venice,* http://shakespeare.mit.edu/merchant/full.html.

Siegel, Daniel J. *Mind: A Journey to the Heart of Being Human*, New York: W.W. Norton, 2017.

Slote, Michael, *The Ethics of Care and Empathy*, London and New York: Routledge, 2007.

Spillius, Elizabeth Bott (ed.), *Melanie Klein Today, Volume 1: Mainly Theory*, London and New York: Routledge, 2000.

Stone, Suzanne Last, "Justice, Mercy and Gender in Rabbinic Thought," *Law and Literature,* vol. 8, no. 1, 1996, pp.139-177.

Wiesel, Elie, *A Jew Today*, New York: Random House, 1978.

Zoloth, Laurie, *Health Care and the Ethics of Encounter: A Jewish Discussion of Social Justice,* Chapel Hill: University of North Carolina Press, 1999.

Zornberg, Avivah Gottleib, *The Beginning of Desire: Reflections on Genesis*, Philadelphia: Jewish Publication Society, 1995.

_____, *Moses: A Human Life*, New Haven: Yale University Press, 2016.

INDEX

A

Aaron   63
Abraham   3, 4, 6, 27, 33, 35, 62, 72
Aggadah   12, 13, 44
Ainsworth, Mary   20, 21, 63
Aquinas   9
Aristotle   10, 22, 27
Artson, Bradley Shavit   40
Attachment   20, 21, 63-65
    Secure attachment   7, 14, 21, 64
Augustine   9
Autonomy   6, 7, 51-54, 56, 57

B

Balaam   55, 57
Bialik, Haim Nahman and Ravnitzky,
Yehoshua   50, 58, 68
Bible   2, 3, 5, 9, 12, 13, 30, 31, 33, 34,
42, 44, 54, 61, 63, 64, 69, 70
    Hebrew Bible   5, 12, 28, 31, 38, 39
    Christian study   5
Bowlby, John   20, 21, 63

C

Calvin, John   9
Campbell, Joseph   1
Care Ethics   1, 5, 16, 21, 23, 51, 72
Chodorow, Nancy   5, 21, 22, 52
Clark, Gordon   31

D

Damasio, Antonio   24
Dawkins, Richard   2, 6
Din   6, 41, 47, 65, 66

E

Eliezer   32,
    Rabbi   43, 54,
    Abraham's servant   32
Elisha   31
Empathy   7, 19, 24, 54, 57, 60-62,
64-66, 69, 70
Encyclopedia Judaica   39, 40, 46
Erikson, Erik   6
Ezer k'negdo   61

F

Fairbairn, Ronald   17
Feminism   1, 5
    Feminist ethics   5, 25, 66, 70
Forgiveness   46, 48
Freud, Sigmund   6, 16, 17, 18, 22, 23,
Friedell, Steven   26, 50
Frymer-Kensky, Tikva   32, 34, 37

G

Gemilut Hasidim   31, 34
Gender differences   22
    Moral thinking   16, 22, 59, 72
Geneivat Da'at   56
Genesis   11, 12, 38, 42, 72
    Breshet (Bereshet, B'reshet)   11
Gilligan, Carol   5, 16, 21-23, 25, 27,
49, 51, 52, 69, 70, 72
Ginzberg, Louis   32, 37
Going beyond the letter of the law   41,
42, 43, 66, 71

H

Hagar and Ishmael   3
Handelman, Susan   10, 15
Hannah   30, 31
Hartman, Tova   27, 29, 30, 31, 54,
Heschel, Abraham Joshua   2, 27, 33,
Hesed   2, 6, 9, 31-36, 46, 60, 65, 72
Hevrutah study   10, 59
Hillel   11, 12, 52
Hoffman, Martin   65, 66, 67
Holtz, Barry   12, 15
Holzer, Elie   67, 68

I

Iacoboni, Marco   20, 26
Isaac   3, 4, 32, 62

J

Jacobs, Jill   39
Jeptha   43, 44, 45
Jocheved   62, 63

K

Kabbalah   12
Kant, Immanuel   6, 22

Klein, Melanie 17, 26
  Kleinians 17
Kohlberg, Lawrence 22, 23

L
Leah 35
Lester, Julius 49
Levinson, Jon 39
Loew, Yehuda – Maharal 31
Luther, Martin 9

M
Mahler, Margaret 5, 22, 52, 55, 56
Mandela, Nelson 41
Midrash 3, 4, 13, 30, 32, 34, 35, 40,
42, 44-46, 54-56, 60, 63, 64, 69, 71
Midrashim 3, 4, 33, 42
Miriam 62, 63
Mirror Neurons 19, 20, 24, 65
Mishnah 50
Mishpat 6, 31, 38, 41, 47, 65, 66
Moses 7, 10, 12, 34, 62-66
Moses ben Nahman 47, 50
Moyers, Bill 1, 8

N
Nachmanides 42, 47
Naomi 35, 72
Neuroscience 5, 14, 16, 19, 24, 65
Noah 40, 41
Noddings, Nel 68

O
Object-relations theory 5, 14, 16, 19,
24, 55
Ona'at Devarim 6, 29, 30, 36
Oven of Akhnai 29, 53, 57

P
Plato 10, 22,
Psychoanalysis 26, 56,

R
Rachel 34, 35
Rachmanut 2
Rahamim 6, 41, 45, 65
Ramban 61
Ramon, Einat 33, 34, 37
Rashi 11, 45, 46, 61, 64, 68

Rabbi Schlomo Yitzhaki 11
Rebecca 32
Rehem 6, 45
Rosh HaShanah 4
Ruth 32, 72

S
Sacks, Jonathan 28, 57, 58
Sanhedrin 43-45
Sarah 3-5, 67, 70, 72
Self 1, 5-7, 10, 14, 16-22, 24, 25, 34,
49, 51-53, 57, 59, 60, 61, 70
  Relational concept 6
  Self-in-relation 14, 25, 52, 53, 62
Septuagint 2
Shakespeare, William 2
  Merchant of Venice 2
Shammai 11
Shekhinah 3
Shifra and Puah 32
Shofar 4, 5, 71
Shumamite Woman 31
Slote, Michael 24, 57, 65, 66
Sodom and Gomorrah 4
Sotah 40
Splansky, Yael 27, 37
Stone, Suzanne Last 34, 37, 50
Stork 45, 46

T
Talmud 12, 13, 30, 42, 43, 45, 49, 56,
62, 69
Tanakh 12, 26
Tikkun Olam 14
Tohu v'vohu 60, 61
Torah 2-4, 11, 12, 27, 28, 31, 33, 39,
40, 43, 44, 47, 53, 54, 57, 62
Tower of Babel 55, 57
Tsedek 2, 6, 9, 38-41, 47, 49, 60, 65,
66, 69
Tsedakah 41
  Righteousness 6, 9, 38-40

W
Wiesel, Elie 49, 50
Winnicott, Donald 18, 22, 59

Z
Zoloth, Laurie 15, 37, 60
Zornberg, Avivah 11, 31, 32, 60, 64

Manufactured by Amazon.ca
Bolton, ON

40491866R00050